...e for the Third Edition of
Parenting the Strong-Willed Child

"This latest revision of *Parenting the Strong-Willed Child* is the best yet! Writing in a beautifully accessible style, Forehand and Long translate scientific findings on effective child-rearing into straightforward, practical guidance for parents. The masterful blend of troubleshooting (Are you accidentally rewarding unwanted behavior?) and positive planning to avoid problems (Building a positive home environment, collaborating with preschool teachers) makes this book an invaluable resource for all parents of young children."
>—*John R. Weisz, Ph.D., ABPP, President and CEO, Judge Baker Children's Center, and Professor of Psychology, Harvard University*

"This is a truly impressive book that will serve as a significant resource to parents of strong-willed children as well as to the professionals who work with these youngsters. Rex Forehand and Nick Long are skilled at presenting research data and strategies in an easy-to-read, practical, realistic manner. Very importantly, their understanding of and compassion and empathy for challenging children and their families are qualities that are apparent throughout this book."
>—*Robert Brooks, Ph.D., Harvard Medical School, and Co-author of* Raising Resilient Children *and* Raising a Self-Disciplined Child

"Forehand and Long score big on this third edition of their now seminal work on parenting the strong-willed child. Each edition of this work gets better and better as their approach has become more and more seasoned over the years. Based on proven, positive, and practical parenting strategies, a delicate dance between parent and child is brought to life in this edition. This is a 'must' book for parents, grandparents, and practicing clinicians working with young children who display such problematic behaviors. This approach has stood the test of time, and it will enrich the lives of many parents and children both now and into the future."
>—*Thomas H. Ollendick, University Distinguished Professor, and Director, Child Study Center, Virginia Tech*

Parenting the Strong-Willed Child provides an invaluable resource to parents—practical guidance toward better parenting offered by two of the world's leading experts based on the best available research evidence. It is a great resource for any parent who wants to help build stronger relationships with their child and a stronger family."
>—*Bruce E. Compas, Ph.D., Patricia and Rodes Hart Professor, Psychology and Pediatrics, Vanderbilt University*

"An immensely important addition to any collection of books about parenting."
—*Charlotte Johnston, Ph.D.. Professor of Psychology, University of British Columbia*

"The authors have successfully translated complex research theories and findings into a straightforward guide for parents. [It's] written in such a conversational tone that the book is easy to read and to absorb."
—*Kenneth A. Dodge, Ph.D., Director, Center for Child and Family Policy, and Professor of Psychology, Duke University*

"This book will be of enormous benefit to the many parents who find themselves doing daily battle with a willful child. . . . The book reflects the state of art in clinical psychology."
—*Mark R. Dadds, Ph.D., Professor of Psychology, University of New South Wales, Australia*

Praise for Prior Editions of
Parenting the Strong-Willed Child

"This is an excellent book written by two renowned researchers who have a wealth of clinical experience as well as firsthand knowledge of what it is to be parents."
—*E. Gail Tripp, Ph.D., Director of Clinical Training, University of Otago, Dunedin, New Zealand*

"As a psychologist and parent of a strong-willed child, I have taught the principles and techniques described in this book to over two hundred families and utilized them in my own family with considerable success. What has most impressed me has been the follow-up with families fifteen years after they have completed this parenting program. Parents reported satisfaction with the program, an improved relationship with their child, and fewer occurrences of negative child behavior."
—*Cynthia G. Baum, Ph.D., President, Argosy University, Washington, D.C.*

"The material covered in this book is the only approach that I know that rests on a solid empirical base."
—*Gerald Patterson, Ph.D., Senior Research Scientist, Oregon Social Learning Center*

"This book successfully integrates clinic-based strategies in [a] real-world setting, and it is heartily recommended."
—Child Psychology and Psychiatry Review

Parenting the Strong-Willed Child

The Clinically Proven Five-Week Program
for Parents of Two- to Six-Year-Olds

REX FOREHAND, PH.D.
NICHOLAS LONG, PH.D.

THIRD EDITION

New York Chicago San Francisco Lisbon London Madrid Mexico City
Milan New Delhi San Juan Seoul Singapore Sydney Toronto

The **McGraw·Hill** Companies

1 2 3 4 5 6 7 8 9 10 11 12 13 14 15   WFR/WFR   1 9 8 7 6 5 4 3 2 1 0

ISBN 978-0-07-166782-1
MHID   0-07-166782-2

Library of Congress Cataloging-in-Publication Data

Forehand, Rex L. (Rex Lloyd), 1945–
        Parenting the strong-willed child : the clinically proven five-week program for
parents of two- to six-year-olds / Rex Forehand and Nicholas Long. — 3rd ed.
            p.   cm.
        Includes bibliographical references and index.
        ISBN-13: 978-0-07-166782-1 (alk. paper)
        ISBN-10: 0-07-166782-2 (alk. paper)
        1. Problem children—Behavior modification.   2. Child rearing.
    3. Parenting.   I. Long, Nicholas, 1956–.   II. Title.

    HQ773.F67   2010
    649'.64—dc21   2010004359

Interior design by Terry Stone

McGraw-Hill books are available at special quantity discounts to use as premiums and
sales promotions or for use in corporate training programs. To contact a representative,
please e-mail us at bulksales@mcgraw-hill.com.

This book is printed on acid-free paper.

This book is dedicated
to the many parents of
strong-willed children.

"The challenges of parenthood are daunting, but its rewards go to the core of what it means to be human—intimacy, growth, learning, and love."

—Carnegie Corporation

Contents

PART III
Creating a Strong Foundation for Behavior Change   155

PART IV
Solving Some Common Behavior Problems:
Additional Recommendations   231

Preface

Parenting is one of the most difficult tasks that we, as adults, face. While most of us receive training for our occupations, we enter the world of parenting with little instruction or guidance. As a result, we use mainly trial and error in our attempts to be effective parents. Unfortunately, with a strong-willed child, there is little time for trial and error. You need effective parenting skills, and you need them now! The first two editions of this book were well received by parents with strong-willed children and by professionals who work with these parents and their children. Based on the feedback from parents and advances in research, we decided an updated and expanded version of *Parenting the Strong-Willed Child* was due.

In this edition, we make a number of additions, including the following:

- Information about recent research that demonstrates the effectiveness of this book
- Expanded information on how to implement the five-week program for changing strong-willed behavior
- Information on topics such as the importance of play and family meals for a child's adjustment
- Updated information on topics such as ADHD and the influence of electronic media

- Information on teaching your child the skills necessary to become a good reader
- Information on a method to teach your child basic social skills
- Information on addressing behavior problems at preschool/school
- Updated information on Internet sites and books for parents
- References/resources for professionals regarding our program

We have also streamlined several chapters so they are more user-friendly.

Perhaps almost as difficult as parenting a strong-willed child is writing a book about how to parent such a child. You have to believe that you know something that can help these parents through the difficult times. Fortunately, we have spent collectively more than sixty-five (yes, 65!) years developing and evaluating programs for parents of strong-willed children. From the research data we have systematically collected and the reports of the many parents with whom we have worked, we know that the skills we have taught parents have helped them improve their relationships with their children. These skills also have helped these parents decrease their children's problem behaviors associated with being strong-willed and enabled the children to capitalize on the positive aspects of their strong wills.

Beyond our research and clinical work with parents and their strong-willed children, both of us bring to this book the experience of being a parent. This personal experience is no small part of what informs this book. We know that parenting is not easy under the best of conditions. We know the difficulties of applying the parenting skills taught in this book. We know the highs and lows of parenting. We have experienced it all on a personal level, and this has helped us be realistic in our advice about parenting.

Since the first edition of this book, there has been controversy about the extent of a parent's influence on her children. In particular, Judith R. Harris, in her book *The Nurture Assumption: Why Children Turn Out the Way They Do* (Free

Press), questions the importance of the role parenting plays on a child's mental and emotional development. In contrast, we noted in the second edition of this book that our view, as well as that of many other behavioral scientists, is that parents do make a difference. Since the second edition, many research studies have continued to support our view. As we discuss in Chapters 1 and 3, there are many other influences on children's behaviors; nevertheless, parents, particularly for young children, have a major influence.

This edition of the book could not have been written without the diligent work of many people. Several people in particular stand out. Robert J. McMahon has served as a guiding light and a wonderful colleague in much of our efforts to understand, implement, and disseminate our parenting programs. He is the senior author of the clinical program, *Helping the Noncompliant Child: Family-Based Treatment of Oppositional Behavior* (Guilford Press), on which this book is based. With patience and constant encouragement, Irene Knight typed and retyped numerous versions of the manuscript. Without her, there would not be a revised and updated edition!

We also want to express our appreciation to Fiona Sarne at McGraw-Hill for the support, encouragement, and feedback she provided. Her skills go far beyond those typically associated with being an editor. We also want to thank Nancy Hall, Judith McCarthy, and the other staff members at McGraw-Hill for their valuable contributions.

As you will read throughout this book, the support, love, and learning that come from a family should never be underestimated. This is certainly the case for both authors. Since the first and second editions of this book, our children have grown up, and one is a parent herself! We have learned more from our children, as well as from our spouses and parents, about parenting since the first two editions; however, we believe our comments of thanks from the first edition still apply. Thus, we are pleased to repeat them here.

The first author (RF) has been fortunate to have received support, love, and numerous invaluable learning experiences from his parents, Rex and Sara Forehand, and his children,

Laura Forehand Wright and Greg Forehand. Thank you! There may be only one person who fell in love in the first grade, never loved anyone else, had the fortune to marry that person, and has been happily married for forty-four years. I am that person. Lell, thank you for your support, excitement about life, strength to fight difficulties, ability to laugh at the darkest moment, and through your need for change, the introduction of new and higher experiences into our lives. But most important, thank you for your love and for being!

The second author (NL) also has been blessed with a loving and supportive family. I would like to thank my parents, John and Jean Long, for providing wonderful examples of what it means to be loving and caring parents. My brother, Adam Long, who was born when I was fifteen years old, helped me realize how wonderful children are and greatly influenced my decision to pursue a career working with children. I want to thank my own children, Justin and Alex Long, for their continued love and support. I am extremely fortunate to have two such wonderful sons. Finally, I want to thank my wife, Sharon, for being whom I consider the best mother in the world. You have taught me so much through your absolute love of being a parent!

The two authors have a friendship that has spanned thirty years. The writing of each edition of this book, as well as many other professional and personal interactions we have, has deepened this friendship. We have provided each other inspiration, support, and positive reinforcement. Indeed, we are fortunate to have each other as friends and to have had the opportunity to share this writing experience.

Introduction

Parents of young strong-willed children are frustrated! They are frustrated by their children's behavior as well as the lack of support and resources to help them deal with their strong-willed children. If you are one of these parents, you are not alone. Most important, there is a strategy for dealing with the negative aspects of your child's strong-willed behavior.

We have spent years developing, evaluating, and using a clinical treatment program that addresses the behavior problems often seen in young children who are very strong-willed, especially problems of not obeying their parents. We developed this program to help parents of these children, focusing on teaching parents techniques that they can use to improve their children's behavior.

Over the past forty years, we and many other researchers around the country have studied this clinical program, and the research has shown the program to be highly effective. Typical results for families who complete the program include improved parent-child relationships (more positive interactions between parent and child), children who mind their parents more, and fewer child behavior problems at home and, sometimes, in other settings such as preschool. Researchers who have done follow-up studies of children up to fifteen years after completion of the clinical program have found the positive results to be lasting.

Because this program is so effective, we have written about it in many professional journals and books. We also have taught the program's parenting techniques to psychologists and other professionals around the country so that they can use it with the parents with whom they work.

We are committed to helping as many families as possible. That is why we decided to initially write and again revise this book for parents. *Parenting the Strong-Willed Child* covers most of the parenting techniques included in our clinical program. We believe that many parents can learn these clinically proven techniques by reading this book and following its recommendations and exercises. If you use these parenting techniques correctly, they will improve your relationship with your child and reduce many of the problems associated with your child's strong-willed behavior.

Two published studies provide support for our conclusion that reading this book can change your child's strong-willed behaviors. In an independent research study, Dr. Nicola Conners at the University of Arkansas for Medical Sciences and her collaborators found that participation in a parenting group that used *Parenting the Strong-Willed Child* as the curriculum was associated with less parenting stress, use of more effective parenting behaviors, and fewer child behavior problems. And, more directly related to you reading this book, the two authors and two of our colleagues, Mary Jane Merchant and Emily Garai, found that parents who read *Parenting the Strong-Willed Child* reported significant decreases in their child's behavior problems. For specific strong-willed behaviors, these parents reported significantly greater decreases than did parents who read a more general parenting book on understanding three- to six-year-old children and their development. However, *Parenting the Strong-Willed Child* was more effective only if parents reported reading most or all of the chapters on implementing the five-week program (Chapters 5 through 11). Not surprisingly, this means you must actually read this book if you expect to change your strong-willed child's behavior. (The complete citation for each of the two studies is in the Appendix under the "References/Resources for Professionals" section.)

We also should note that *Parenting the Strong-Willed Child* has received the Association for Behavioral and Cognitive Therapies Book of Merit Award. The award is given for educating the general public about the benefits of psychological treatments that have been proven to work. The five-week program described in this book can improve your child's behavior!

While this book is based on our clinical program, it is not a substitute for individual professional help if your child has severe behavior problems or if he might have a disorder such as hyperactivity (officially known as *attention deficit/hyperactivity disorder*). (See Chapter 4, "Does My Child Have ADHD?") If your child is exhibiting severe problems, we recommend that you consult your child's physician or a mental health professional for evaluation and assistance. The Association for Behavioral and Cognitive Therapies (abct.org) can help you find a therapist. However, even for many of the families that need professional guidance, we believe that the techniques presented in this book can be helpful as a supplement.

Overview of the Book

Our strategy for addressing strong-willed behavior has three dimensions. The first dimension involves helping you understand your child's strong-willed behavior and how various factors influence such behavior. The second utilizes specific parenting techniques for addressing the behavior problems most commonly exhibited by strong-willed children who are two to six years old. The third seeks to help you foster a strong foundation within your family and home that will make these parenting techniques most effective. When combined, these three dimensions form a holistic strategy you can use to understand your child's behavior and to learn how to change it.

The book is divided into four parts. Each of the first three parts describes a different dimension of our strategy for parenting. The fourth part describes how to combine what you have learned from the previous three parts, along with other practical suggestions, to manage specific behavior problems. Part I explains the factors that cause or contribute to your child's strong-willed behavior. We start by examining the role of temperament in setting the stage for strong-willed behavior. We then address how your reactions to your child's behavior can affect and sometimes actually increase this behavior. We then go on to consider how factors such as conflict with your spouse (or ex-spouse), divorce, your mood, alcohol abuse, and electronic media affect a child's behavior. Finally, as parents often have difficulty differentiating strong-willed behavior from attention deficit/hyperactivity disorder, we end this part with a chapter addressing this issue.

The parenting techniques in Part II take the form of a five-week program for dealing with the behavior problems associated with a child being strong-willed. You will learn and practice a new skill every week. By the end of the five weeks, you should notice a significant improvement in your relationship with your child and in your child's behavior.

In Part III, we focus on ways to develop a more positive atmosphere in your family and home. The purpose of this part is to enhance and maintain the positive behavior changes that occurred as a result of the five-week program. The chapters in this part explain how you can improve your family life, improve your communication skills, develop greater patience in dealing with your child, boost your child's self-esteem, and teach your child basic social skills.

Part IV offers strategies for managing specific behavior problems commonly reported by parents of young strong-willed children. Each problem is addressed separately, and the recommendations supplement the parenting skills discussed in Parts II and III.

In this edition, we include an appendix listing a number of websites where you can obtain further information on parenting. We also include a list of books parents may find beneficial and a brief list of references to research on our program that professionals may find helpful.

Since *Parenting the Strong-Willed Child* was first published, the role of ethnicity or race in parenting has been more thoroughly studied. The studies that have appeared suggest that a parent's cultural background does affect her beliefs about parenting and child behavior, as well as parenting itself. However, strong-willed child behavior and parenting difficulties appear to exist in families of most ethnic groups. Furthermore, the same parenting techniques—those presented in this book—are effective for parents of most ethnic groups. You may need to adapt them slightly based on your cultural background, but the basic principles of the program are effective in parenting most strong-willed children.

In a similar way, research on the father's role in the family has increased in recent years. In some families, fathers may use parenting skills at different levels or intensities than mothers; however, what is most important is for fathers to be actively involved in parenting and, to the extent possible, for mothers' and fathers' parenting to be consistent. When possible, both parents should read this book and work together to change their strong-willed child's behavior. If this is not possible, this approach can still be effective when used by a single parent.

We hope that this book will help you understand your strong-willed child's behavior, learn effective parenting skills, and learn how to enhance and maintain these parenting skills. We hope that learning how to use these skills, along with other recommendations that we offer to effectively address your major concerns regarding your child's behavior, will, in turn, increase your sense of competence as a parent.

Authors' Note: *In referring to children, we decided to use masculine pronouns for ease and clarity, not to imply that girls cannot be as strong-willed as boys. For the same reasons of convenience, we use primarily feminine pronouns when referring to parents.*

PART I

Understanding Your Strong-Willed Child's Behavior

As parents, we can do a better job of addressing strong-willed behavior if we understand what it is and where it comes from. If you understand what factors contribute to your child's behavior, you will be better able to make the changes needed to address undesirable behavior. In Part I, we give our views on the role of temperament in determining your child's behavior (Chapter 1), how your responses to your child's behavior can actually increase his strong-willed behavior (Chapter 2), how various factors within and outside the family affect your child's behavior (Chapter 3), and how you can tell the difference between strong-willed behavior and attention deficit/hyperactivity disorder (Chapter 4).

1

Strong-Willed Behavior and How It All Begins

"**H**e was born with a strong will!" That was what Tommy's parents told us when he was two years old. Several hours after Tommy was born, they said, the hospital nurses told them how fussy he was. Tommy cried and cried and cried. His parents thought it was colic and that his crying would decrease as he grew older. Unfortunately, as the months passed, the crying and fussing continued. By eighteen months, he was always fussing and crying to get his way or to show he did not like something. He would fuss and cry when he had to take a bath or get dressed. Going to bed and getting up led to more fussing. It was not pleasant!

Four-year-old Johnny was very outgoing and independent. Unfortunately, he was also very demanding. His parents and his preschool teacher stated that he was "as stubborn as they come." If he did not get his way, Johnny would become upset and have temper tantrums. These tantrums included yelling, crying, and stomping his feet. Johnny was also very active and intense. He always was on the go and filled with boundless energy. As a result of his activity level, he often fell down. Although he rarely hurt himself, he would scream and act as if he had been mortally wounded.

Mary was a six-year-old kindergartner. Testing at school indicated that she had above-average intelligence and academic skills. She was also very confident and would persevere in challenging activities long after most other children gave up. Mary had never minded her parents very well but did follow her teacher's instructions at preschool. Unfortunately, when she went to first grade, Mary began not minding at school. At first Mary would just ignore instructions her teacher gave her. Then she became openly defiant, saying, "No, I will not do it!" in response to instructions from her teacher. Mary's parents were concerned that her behavior would affect her future education.

What Is Strong-Willed Behavior?

The parents of Tommy, Johnny, and Mary all considered their child to be strong-willed. But what does being strong-willed really mean? From our experience, these children usually have a very strong sense of independence. In many ways this is very positive because individuals who are independent are typically also assertive, confident, determined, and persistent. Unfortunately, a strong sense of independence also frequently leads these young children to become stubborn, argumentative, and defiant. To see whether parents agreed with our view of the characteristics associated with being a "strong-willed child," we conducted a survey. We asked a group of parents of two- to six-year-old children, who were enrolled in a parenting class, to tell us whether or not their child was strong-willed and what they believed were the characteristics of being strong-willed. An amazing 48 percent of the parents reported that their young child was "strong-willed." To read how they described those children, see the box titled "Is Your Child Strong-Willed?" later in this chapter.

A strong-willed child can be very frustrating and challenging to a parent (as you probably well know!). However, both positive and negative qualities are associated with being strong-willed. The key is to nurture your strong-willed child's positive qualities while minimizing the impact of the negative qualities on him—and on others.

If you are like most parents of strong-willed children, your child's strong will may continually conflict with what you, as his parent, believe is best for him and your family. If this is the case, you will need to work with him to direct his strong will in more positive ways. The purpose of this book is to help you do this. You will decrease the negative aspects of your child's strong will while encouraging him to use it in positive ways. We hope that your child will learn to use his strong will to excel in life.

In the Beginning There Was Temperament

How does a child become strong-willed? Many of the characteristics of being strong-willed have their roots in a child's temperament. As you will read in Chapters 2 and 3, a child's temperament lays the groundwork for his behavior and then interacts with a number of factors, particularly parenting, to lead to behavior that can be labeled strong-willed. This chapter will focus on helping you understand temperament and its relationship to the behavior of children and their parents.

Temperament generally refers to a child's inborn behavioral style or innate tendencies to act a certain way. Temperament is reflected in how a child typically approaches, interacts in, and experiences social relationships. Imagine two fifteen-month-old children who fall down while running across a lawn. Neither child is injured, but one child screams and cries following the fall. The other child laughs after he falls, gets up, and starts to run again. The different ways these children handle the fall reflect, in part, their temperaments.

Temperament is generally considered to be something with which you are born. Many professionals believe that a child's basic temperament can be seen in early infancy, well

Is Your Child Strong-Willed?

If your child is strong-willed, you probably have known it since he was a baby! These are the children who feel their wants and needs strongly, and they let you know just how they feel. A group of parents in a parenting class described their own strong-willed children in the following terms:

- "If she doesn't want to do something, there is no way you can make her do it"
- "Always wanting to do everything for herself"
- "Demands constant attention"
- "Always wanting to make the decisions/choices"
- "Not recognizing authority of adults/parents"
- "Persistent"
- "Unpredictable"
- "Stubborn"
- "Independent"
- "Determined"
- "Temperamental"
- "Bad temper"
- "Talks back a lot"
- "Overly sensitive"
- "Frequent temper tantrums"
- "Negative reactions—everything is a fight or a struggle"
- "Won't mind"
- "Resists direction"
- "Doesn't respond to discipline"
- "Knows no limits"
- "Tells us what to do"
- "Very outgoing"

- "Resists anything done to him—diaper changes, bath, dressing, etc."
- "Headstrong"
- "Argumentative"
- "Aggressive"
- "Often upset"
- "Dominant"
- "Confident"
- "Questioning"
- "Assertive"
- "Completes a task in her own way even if you show an easier way the task can be completed"
- "Cries to get her way constantly"
- "Her way or no way—no matter what"
- "Argues every point"
- "Pushes things to the extreme"
- "Works on a frustrating task (one that may be over his age level) until completed"
- "Will focus on one thing and be persistent until she gets what she wants"
- "Has own ideas"
- "Resistant to change"

Do any of these descriptions sound like your child? If so, you have a lot of company!

before a particular parenting style has had time to have a major impact on his behavior. However, as we will show you later, your child's actual behavior (for example, what he does when told "no") is a function of both his temperament and your parenting.

Researchers have identified numerous temperament traits. A child's overall temperament is the combination of these individual traits. While there is not a pure "strong-willed temperament," there are several traits that are seen in many strong-willed children. These temperament traits include reactivity (how intensely a child reacts, either positively or negatively, to different situations or events), adaptability (how well a child adapts to changes in situations and events), persistence (how long a child stays with an activity), and emotionality (the stability and the positive/negative aspects of a child's mood or emotions). Strong-willed children are more likely than other children to react intensely, to have a difficult time adapting to transitions, to be persistent when they want to have their own way, and to have inconsistent moods.

In summary, there are several specific temperament traits that we frequently observe in strong-willed children. This observation leads to the next question: are these early temperament traits associated with later behavior problems?

According to a number of research studies, a child's early temperament is significantly related to his later behavior. For example, infants and toddlers who are more irritable, restless, and have trouble adapting to new situations tend to have more behavior problems as they get older. Studies have found that difficult temperament in toddlers is strongly related to aggression and behavior problems from at least ages three through twelve. A child's early temperament has been linked not only to later behavior problems but also to later issues in other areas, including peer relationships, preschool adjustment, and even academic achievement. (However, as we will discuss next, most of these same studies indicate that temperament cannot explain the whole story about a child's behavior.)

Temperament, Parenting, and Behavior

Many parents ask us whether it is their child's temperament or their parenting that has "caused" their child's strong-willed behavior. Such a question is like the often-debated question of whether nature or nurture is most important in determining our personality. Since temperament and parenting continually interact, we seldom can know which is more important in determining a child's strong-willed behavior. It is interesting to note that several recent research studies have found that children with difficult temperaments are more affected by parenting practices than children with average or easy temperaments. So, you can make a difference in your child's strong-willed behavior.

What is clear is that temperament and parenting are both important and clearly linked. Research suggests that many of the temperament traits we have been discussing can change as a child develops. That is, many of these temperament traits are not biologically fixed but rather are tendencies that can be modified by parenting style and other environmental factors. As we will discuss in Chapter 2, we believe that strong-willed children typically have certain temperamental traits that lead to certain parenting practices. These practices, in turn, often strengthen the very strong-willed behaviors that parents want to decrease. This is good news because it means your strong-willed child's behavior is not biologically "fixed" by his temperament! You can influence your child's behavior through your parenting practices. Our five-week program for parents (Part II of this book) lays out parenting practices that will decrease the likelihood of later behavior problems in children with difficult temperaments.

In summary, strong-willed behavior is common among young children and often has its roots in a child's early temperament. However, you *can* change the negative aspects of your child's strong-willed behavior through your parenting. In fact, that is probably why you bought this book!

2

Why Is My Child Becoming Even More Strong-Willed?

The evidence suggests that many children are born with a strong-willed disposition, and this is not necessarily good or bad. However, a young strong-willed child is more likely to engage in more of the negative behaviors we associate with a strong will—such as stubbornness, impatience, and tantrums. When that happens, strong-willed behavior becomes a problem. And a key factor that determines whether the child's behavior becomes more problematic is the way the parents manage the behavior.

If your child's behavior is becoming worse, don't simply blame yourself. The way you have been responding to your child's behavior has been, in part, a function of his behavior. Unfortunately, strong-willed children often bring out the worst in parents. Responding in a positive way to a child who has an easy temperament is relatively easy. In contrast, when faced with the frustrations of dealing with a strong-willed child, parents are much more likely to use less-than-ideal parenting strategies.

The focus of this chapter is how your child's behavior affects the way you respond to it and how your response, in turn, affects his behavior. We will start by discussing ways children learn to behave through their interactions with others. Our goal is to give you a basic understanding of how a child's behavior develops as a result of the environment in which he lives. This will help you analyze and solve the problem behaviors of your strong-willed child.

Learning Through Social Interactions

Much of how a child behaves is learned from interactions with others, which has been termed *social learning*. Temperament and other factors lay the groundwork, but it is through social learning that children establish most specific behaviors, both appropriate and inappropriate. Social learning occurs in three major ways: through modeling, reinforcement, and punishment.

Modeling

This aspect of social learning is basically learning by example. *Modeling* occurs when a child learns how to behave a certain way by observing others behaving that way. Your child may see another child having a tantrum because the child wants a cookie. If the other child receives the cookie after the tantrum, your child learns, by observation, that a tantrum may be an effective way to get something. The next time your child wants something, he is more likely to have a tantrum.

Observing someone behave in a certain way does not mean your child will automatically behave that way, but it does increase the chances that he might. Whether your child will imitate someone depends on many things, including whether he wants to be like that other person, how many times he observes the behavior, and whether the behavior observed had a positive outcome (like the child receiving the cookie to stop the tantrum).

Modeling is a very important and powerful way of learning. You need to make sure that the behavior you model for your child is appropriate. Since young children look up to their parents, they are especially likely to behave like their parents do. For example, losing your temper in front of your child when you become frustrated increases the chance that your child will handle frustration in a similar way. Children often look to their parents for examples of how to behave in difficult situations. The philosophy "Do as I say, not as I do" does not work. Modeling is more powerful than words in teaching children how to behave. Set a good example for your child! If you are strong-willed yourself, try to model the positive behaviors associated with being strong-willed, not the negative ones. For example, when you are upset with someone, try to model appropriate assertiveness, not aggressiveness. Model persistence when you face challenging tasks. Let your child see you keep doing something difficult until you are successful.

Reinforcement

When most people think of *reinforcement*, they tend to think of giving children things like candy or money for good behavior. Such an understanding is immensely oversimplified and does not do the principle justice. Although many people resist the notion, reinforcement guides much of our behavior. In fact, it is a major key to the development of our child's behavior. The principle of reinforcement is simply that if a behavior is followed by something positive, the behavior is more likely to occur in the future.

We are not saying a child's social behavior is primarily guided by someone's giving him material things whenever he behaves in certain ways. Most reinforcers are social in nature. These *social reinforcers*—attention, smiles, laughter, and so on—have the greatest impact on your behavior and on your child's behavior. Much of your child's behavior is gradually established through social reinforcers that occur over and over again each day. No single reinforcer will have a dramatic impact on behavior. Reinforcers work slowly and have to occur repeatedly in order to really change a person's behavior.

Think about situations in your life in which social reinforcers guide your behavior. For example, you are more likely to talk to someone who smiles at you as you approach her than to someone who looks away. This is usually because your past experiences have been positive when you talked to individuals who smiled at you. Similarly, you probably spend more time talking to someone who gives you attention and makes you laugh. Your talking is being reinforced by the attention and laughing. In the same way, your child is reinforced more by little (but frequently occurring) responses to him, such as a touch, a smile, a compliment, a positive glance, or a word of encouragement, than by material rewards such as toys, candy, or money. A parent who gives a lot of social reinforcement to her child tends to receive a lot of social reinforcement from her child in return. One mother who went through our clinical program told us, "When I started smiling more at my child, he started to smile more at me. It made me feel so good."

Another kind of reinforcement is *negative reinforcement*. Many people confuse negative reinforcement with punishment, but they are not the same. Negative reinforcement, like positive reinforcement, strengthens behavior. However, in negative reinforcement, a behavior is reinforced not because it results in something positive but because it results in the removal or end of something negative. Suppose your child is playing in a sandbox. Another child begins throwing sand, which blows into your child's face. Your child goes over to the other child and assertively says, "Stop throwing the sand." If the other child stops throwing the sand, your child's assertiveness will have been negatively reinforced. That is, your child's assertiveness was followed by the end of something negative (blowing sand). Your child's assertiveness is strengthened, and he is more likely to be assertive in the future. Negative reinforcement can be difficult to fully understand, but it is important. It can play a major role in the development of disruptive behavior, as we will discuss later in this chapter.

Punishment

Whereas reinforcement strengthens behavior, *punishment* weakens behavior. In the minds of many parents, punishment means spanking. However, spanking is only one type of punishment and, as research shows, not a particularly good type when long-term outcomes are considered. Punishment includes time-outs, reprimands, and removal of privileges. Anything that follows a behavior and weakens it is punishment.

Although a single punishment rarely leads to any long-term changes in behavior, punishment can be effective if used correctively and consistently. However, relying too much on punishment has the following drawbacks:

- Punishment gives a child the message of what not to do without necessarily teaching what to do.
- To maintain the effectiveness of punishment, parents often have to use increasingly harsher punishment. If punishment becomes significantly more frequent and intense over time, it can lead to problems such as child abuse.
- With frequent punishment, a child may resent his parent and become aggressive toward her.
- Individuals who give a lot of punishment tend to receive a lot of punishment in return.

As with reinforcement, you tend to receive what you give. For example, parents who use excessive punishment frequently find themselves on the receiving end of their child's anger.

In summary, using some types of punishment, such as time-out, sparingly and along with a lot of reinforcement for positive behavior can be effective. However, excessive use of punishment may create more problems than it solves.

Accidentally Reinforcing Your Child's Inappropriate Behavior

Although much of your child's social learning takes place through reinforcement, you may often provide the reinforcement without being aware of it. This unintended reinforcement occurs naturally within everyday interactions.

Unfortunately, you often end up reinforcing the exact behaviors you are trying to eliminate.

Sometimes a parent inadvertently rewards her child's inappropriate behavior. For example, when you are shopping with your child, he sees a toy he wants. He starts to cry and whine. You try to comfort and calm him. Still whining and crying, he asks you again for the toy. You hate to see him upset or you are embarrassed by his behavior, so you agree to buy the toy for him. What has happened in this interaction? You rewarded your child for crying and fussing by providing attention and comfort, as well as by purchasing the toy. What has your child learned? He has learned that he can sometimes get your attention and what he wants by crying and fussing. The next time he wants something, what is he more likely to do? Cry and whine in an effort to get what he wants. We call this the *positive reinforcement trap*—we as parents reinforce and increase the likelihood of the very behavior we want to decrease. To better understand this concept, see additional examples in "Are You Rewarding the Behaviors You Don't Like?" on the next page.

A single incident like the preceding example will not permanently affect your child's behavior. However, when this type of interaction occurs repeatedly, it can lead to an escalation of crying, fussing, or other inappropriate behaviors. Since you surely don't want to reward your child's inappropriate behavior, analyze your own behavior. Are you unintentionally rewarding your child's inappropriate behavior? If so, try to stop. If you find it extremely difficult to stop, do not be surprised. Old habits are hard to change. The parenting program presented in Part II will help you escape the positive reinforcement trap.

Children also learn to misbehave in order to avoid something they do not like. For example, you tell your child to pick up the toys that he has left on the floor. He does not pick them up, so you start reminding him over and over. Out of frustration, you resort to nagging. As you are nagging him, he turns to you, starts to cry, and calls you "mean" as he runs to his

Are You Rewarding the Behaviors You Don't Like?

In spite of our best intentions as parents, we often reinforce the very behaviors we most want to end. Have you ever responded to your child's behavior in any of the following ways?

- Repeatedly responding to your child's calls after he has gone to bed
- Comforting your child when he has a tantrum
- Giving attention to your child each time he interrupts your conversation with another adult
- Laughing at your child's inappropriate behavior
- Giving your child candy in the grocery store when he starts crying
- Letting your child sleep with you every night just because he begs to do so

If you have done these things, you have fallen into the positive reinforcement trap. You are encouraging the inappropriate behavior by rewarding it with attention, comfort, laughter, and so on.

Many parents also fall prey to the negative reinforcement trap. Do any of these actions sound familiar?

- Letting your child skip his bath because he cries when you say "bath time"
- Telling your child to get out of the bathtub but, because he cries, letting him stay in longer
- Letting your child leave an event because he begs not to stay and has a tantrum
- Canceling the babysitter because your child cries when you tell him you are going out
- Telling your child to sit quietly at the dinner table but, because he has a tantrum, letting him leave the table
- Taking your child out of his car seat because he cries to get out

These responses to negative behavior reinforce the behavior by ending something your child perceived as unpleasant, such as taking a bath or having a babysitter.

Fortunately, there is an escape from both of these traps. The details are in Part II.

room. You decide that it's just not worth the frustration to make him pick up the toys. You pick up the toys and put them away. What happened in this situation? Well, your child learned that by crying, calling you a name, and running away from you, he made you stop the nagging and he did not have to pick up the toys. This is an example of the *negative reinforcement trap*. As with the positive reinforcement trap, this trap reinforces and increases the likelihood of the behavior a parent wants to decrease. More examples are given in the box "Are You Rewarding the Behaviors You Don't Like?" to help you understand the negative reinforcement trap.

Just as with the positive reinforcement trap, a single incident involving negative reinforcement will not permanently affect your child's behavior. However, when this type of interaction occurs repeatedly, it can lead to a significant escalation in inappropriate behaviors.

The Coercive Process

A negative reinforcement trap rarely occurs in isolation. Complex interactions between a parent and child often involve both individuals falling into the negative reinforcement trap. Gerald Patterson, an internationally renowned researcher at the Oregon Social Learning Center, has studied this phenomenon extensively and has identified what he calls the *coercive process*. This process occurs in many families with a young child who is strong-willed. The coercive process can occur repeatedly during the hundreds of interactions between a parent and child each week. As a result, a child's behavior and the parent's management of the behavior gradually become more and more negative as each person's behavior receives frequent negative reinforcement.

As an example of the coercive process, imagine you take your child to a store and tell him to hold your hand. He does not want to hold your hand, so he starts whining and trying to pull away to escape your grasp. Out of frustration, you eventually give up and let go of his hand so that you do not have to deal with his fussiness and constant tugging. In this

The Coercive Process

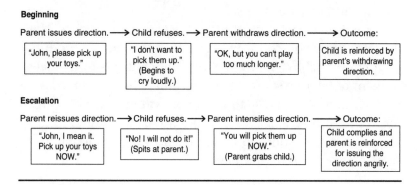

Beginning

Parent issues direction. ⟶ Child refuses. ⟶ Parent withdraws direction. ⟶ Outcome:

| "John, please pick up your toys." | "I don't want to pick them up." (Begins to cry loudly.) | "OK, but you can't play too much longer." | Child is reinforced by parent's withdrawing direction. |

Escalation

Parent reissues direction. ⟶ Child refuses. ⟶ Parent intensifies direction. ⟶ Outcome:

| "John, I mean it. Pick up your toys NOW." | "No! I will not do it!" (Spits at parent.) | "You will pick them up NOW." (Parent grabs child.) | Child complies and parent is reinforced for issuing the direction angrily. |

situation, his fussing and resistance to your direction to hold your hand were negatively reinforced by your giving in to him. But your giving in also was negatively reinforced, because it stopped his fussing and resistance. As a result of this interaction, your child will more likely resist you and fuss to get his way in the future. And, you will more likely give in to his resistance and fussiness because by giving in before, you stopped the problems in the short run.

Now let's add a different twist to the same example. In this case, when your child whines and physically resists holding your hand, you raise your voice and tell him that he has to hold your hand. The resistance continues and, in fact, becomes worse. You lose your temper and start yelling at him. He stops resisting. In this case, your yelling was negatively reinforced because it stopped the resistance. This will increase the chances that you will yell at him again in the future.

With the coercive processes described here, a child's behavior gradually becomes more negative, and a parent's response to the negative behavior gradually becomes more severe. For example, your child's temper tantrums or other negative behaviors might become more intense and frequent, while at the same time you start to yell or spank more intensely and frequently. This downward cycle will continue as you are each reinforced for use of increasingly negative behavior. How are you reinforced? By the termination of the other person's negative behavior. "The Coercive Process" figure above illustrates a common interaction between a strong-willed child and his parent.

The coercive process is difficult to grasp all at once. However, we hope you can appreciate that the way you manage your child's behavior can play a significant role in the development of later problems. The way you behave influences his behavior now—and also the way you will manage his behavior in the future. This effect occurs not as a result of isolated incidents but through an ongoing series of complex interactions between a parent and child.

Other Factors That Contribute to Strong-Willed Behavior Problems

Besides the positive reinforcement trap and the negative reinforcement trap (which escalates in the coercive process), several other factors may lead to your child's becoming increasingly strong-willed. Parents who have children with behavior problems tend to pay less attention to their child's positive behaviors. These parents become so frustrated in having to deal with their child's negative behaviors that they have a hard time noticing and acknowledging the behaviors that are positive. As the parent of a strong-willed child, you need to make an extra effort to acknowledge and praise your child's positive behaviors. Make sure you let your child know that you notice the times he does do what you tell him. We will discuss this issue in greater detail in Parts II and III.

Parents of strong-willed children also are often uncertain how to manage their child's disruptive behavior. This uncertainty can result in an inconsistent pattern of discipline. A parent who feels overwhelmed and questions her ability to manage her child's disruptive behavior may withdraw from the situation and not intervene at all. At other times she may become frustrated and resort to overly aggressive ways of managing her child's disruptive behavior—for example, losing her temper and yelling or spanking. Neither an overly permissive nor an aggressive parenting style is very effective. In fact, these styles tend to escalate behavior problems, especially when used inconsistently. The five-week parenting program presented in Part II can help you become a more positive and consistent parent.

Modeling is one of the most powerful forms of teaching both positive and negative behaviors. If your strong-willed child is frequently around other children who often misbehave, he may start to copy their negative behaviors. This will be especially true if your child does not observe an adult effectively managing the other children's misbehavior. Take charge and create an environment that is positive for your child. Arrange play situations with friends who do not feed your child's negative behavior. Try to encourage him to interact with children who are generally well behaved. Just like bad behavior, good behavior will rub off!

Children also model the behavior of their parents, as we discussed earlier in this chapter. If you frequently yell when frustrated, your child will learn to yell when he becomes frustrated. If you hit when angry, your child will learn to hit when he becomes angry. On the positive side, if you model appropriate behavior, your child likely will behave more appropriately. When you become frustrated or angry, try to stay calm and model appropriate ways of handling the situation. The important point is to remember to set a good example for your child.

The negative behaviors we associate with being strong-willed may become more pronounced if your child does not get enough sleep. Tired children often are fussy. The fussiness can trigger the negative interactions associated with the coercive process. As a result, the fussiness may contribute to behavior problems as the parent and child become increasingly negative with one another. If your child is not getting enough sleep, there are several things that you can do. For some suggestions, see Part IV.

Reasons Children Become Increasingly Strong-Willed	TABLE 2-1

- Positive reinforcement trap
- Negative reinforcement trap
- Coercive process (repeated negative reinforcement traps set by parent and child)
- Child receives little attention for positive behavior
- Parent is inconsistent in response to behavior problems
- Child's peers model inappropriate behavior
- Parents model inappropriate behavior
- Child lacks adequate rest

If your child is increasingly engaging in negative behaviors associated with having a strong will, Table 2-1 may help. It summarizes the reasons for a child becoming increasingly strong-willed. Might some of these apply to you and your child? If so, this book has many ideas to improve your parenting skills and your child's behavior.

3

It Takes More than Just Good Parenting

Good parenting skills alone cannot guarantee that your child will always behave as you wish. Besides your child's temperament and your parenting techniques, many other things can influence your child's behavior. Among the most important are problems that put stress on families. In this chapter, we will briefly examine how five sources of family stress—divorce, remarriage, conflict, depressed mood, or alcohol abuse—can affect parenting and children's behavior. The figure "Family Stress, Parenting, and Your Child's Behavior" presents a model showing that each of these factors and others can create stress that can directly—or indirectly, through parenting—affect children's behavior. We also will consider one other influence on your child's behavior: screen time (this includes television, video games, and computer use).

These five sources of family stress and screen time can have negative effects on your child, but you have some ability to limit those effects. This chapter will explain how. We also refer you to one of our other books, *Making Divorce Easier on Your Child: 50 Effective Ways to Help Children Adjust* (McGraw-Hill), for ideas on how to address three of the family stressors: divorce, remarriage, and conflict with your spouse or ex-spouse. As most parents experience depressed

Family Stress, Parenting, and Your Child's Behavior

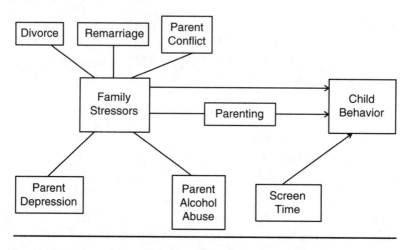

moods and as there is a lot of recent research on how these moods and clinical depression can affect children, we will explore this topic in more detail. Similarly, as many parents drink alcohol, we will examine this topic and make recommendations to you. Finally, exposure to screen time, whether through television, computer games, or the Internet, is increasing for all of us. It is important for us to point out how screen time can impact our children and to make some suggestions about how parents can best deal with this influence.

Of course, many other stressors, including economic hardship, work problems, physical illness, and abuse of drugs (other than alcohol), also can be family stressors. We focus on the five stressors discussed in this chapter as examples in order to give you a broad understanding of how such stressors can affect children. We selected these five stressors and screen time because ample research has examined their impact on children.

Divorce

Every year more than a million children in the United States experience parental divorce. Based on current divorce trends, about 30 percent of children born today will experience a parental divorce before they reach age eighteen. Divorce and single-parent families have become a way of life in our society.

Research indicates that divorce can have a negative impact on the behavior of children; however, this impact is not nearly as great as the public media often report. Also, some evidence suggests that the behavior of preschool children improves over the two years following divorce. Most important to note is that many of the problems children have following parental divorce are not simply a result of the separation of their parents. To a large extent, children's adjustment following parental divorce depends on the situation existing after the divorce. Fortunately, you as a parent often can control many aspects of the situation that may affect your child's adjustment. As the title suggests, our book *Making Divorce Easier on Your Child: 50 Effective Ways to Help Children Adjust* presents fifty ways you can help your child before, during, and after a divorce. If you and your spouse are considering divorce or have already divorced, we encourage you to read the book. It will give you many ways to help you minimize the negative effects of divorce on your child. For example, it is critical that you do not argue in front of your child or enlist him as your ally in disagreements with your ex-spouse.

Remarriage

Most parents who divorce will remarry in the next five years. Like divorce, remarriage is becoming a way of life in American society. Remarriage puts parents in a challenging situation. You have to develop the new marriage within the context of the relationship you have with your child and your ex-spouse. Also, your new spouse will bring into the marriage his or her kinships, possibly including his or her children. You have to form workable relationships with these people. You need to help define and develop the parenting role to be played by the new spouse.

As with divorce, the remarriage itself is often less important to the child than how the parents handle the situation. You can help your child adjust to this family change by reading Chapter 47 on dating and Chapter 48 on new family combinations in our book *Making Divorce Easier on Your Child*. Remarriage is not necessarily easy for children; however, with time, love, and good parenting, it can work! These chapters provide a number of recommendations, including the importance of not hiding your dating from your child and, after remarriage, carefully planning what role your new spouse will play in parenting your child.

Conflict

Continued parental conflict in front of your child is more harmful for him than divorce! That doesn't mean you and your spouse should divorce rather than have occasional conflict or that you should never disagree in front of your child. Resolving disagreements in a constructive way may actually serve as an example to him about how to deal with differences of opinion. However, if you and your spouse have frequent hostile conflicts in front of your child, you are modeling inappropriate ways to address differences. Furthermore, your child may feel anxious about what the conflict means (he may think, for example, "My parents hate each other and are going to divorce"). Frequent hostile arguments may also disrupt your ability to parent effectively. Again, our book *Making Divorce Easier on Your Child* has chapters on communicating with your ex-spouse (Chapter 10), not arguing with your ex-spouse in front of your child (Chapter 11), and not using your child as an ally during disputes with your ex-spouse (Chapter 13). Almost all of our recommendations in these chapters apply equally well to married couples. If you engage in frequent conflict with your spouse or ex-spouse, you need to read these chapters!

Clinical Depression and Depressive Mood

It has been estimated that each year depression affects about one in five parents in the United States. This is a major issue as over 15 million children (under eighteen) lived with an adult with clinical depression in the past year. Unfortunately, only one-third of adults with depression get treatment.

Clinical depression typically involves many of the following symptoms:

- Feeling down nearly every day
- Decreased interest in things you used to enjoy
- Significant changes in your appetite and/or weight
- Major changes in how much you sleep
- Feeling tired nearly every day
- Feeling guilty or worthless nearly every day
- Difficulty concentrating and/or making decisions

Clinical depression can have a harmful effect on parenting and on a child. Researchers have found that parental depression increases the risk for emotional and behavioral problems in children.

You may not have clinical depression but just have the blues or depressed moods occasionally. Even these moods can have a negative impact on your child. Your mood can influence how you view his behavior, how you parent, and how he behaves. When you feel down, you may be less understanding and tolerant of your child. As a result, sometimes you may overreact to his problem behaviors and be more negative, harsh, and critical. At other times, you may withdraw and not react at all to your child's behavior. And, at other times you may use guilt to deal with your strong-willed child's behavior (for example, "You make me feel so bad when you act that way!"). Once your mood improves, you may interact more consistently in a positive way with him and enforce rules you have established. In short, as your mood changes, your parenting practices also change, which is confusing for your child. And, as a consequence, his behavior may become more strong-willed.

If you are a person who experiences depression or is often moody, the following guidelines will help minimize the effects on your child:

- **Evaluate your moods.** Do they change frequently? Do you often respond to your child based on your mood? If so, work on developing a positive and consistent mood yourself. If your changing moods do not improve or you have several of the symptoms of clinical depression listed in this chapter, seek professional help. There are many effective treatment options that can make a real difference in your life (and the life of your child).
- **Monitor your moods.** Note what occurs before and during mood change. This can help you identify what influences your moods and may help you address issues related to your moods.
- **Rely on your spouse for co-parenting.** Your spouse can help compensate for parenting difficulties you experience because of your depressive moods. He or she can work on maintaining a good relationship with your child and using good parenting skills.
- **Tell your family members when you are feeling down.** Do not expect them to "read your mood." Ask for their help in making it through the day.
- **Avoid making your child feel guilty or sorry for you.** Research, including our own, indicates that depressed parents often use guilt to control their children (for example, "Why are you always doing things to make me feel so bad?"). As a result, these children experience more depression themselves.
- **Read Chapter 14 of this book carefully.** Many of the issues and recommendations we discuss in that chapter may be especially helpful to you.
- **Work toward consistent parenting.** If you have clear guidelines for yourself as a parent, like those in our five-

week program presented in Chapters 6 through 10 of this book, your parenting will be less influenced by your mood. Also, our research and that of others has shown that changing your parenting and your child's behavior through a program like ours can actually lead to improvements in your mood. As you parent more effectively and your child's strong-willed behavior improves, you may feel better about yourself.

If you do have clinical depression, it is important to realize that your child is at an increased risk for developing depression at some point in his life. Therefore, if your child starts to display symptoms suggestive of depression, you should have him evaluated by a mental health professional.

Alcohol Abuse

Use of alcohol by adults is a well-established and generally accepted part of our society. Most people who choose to drink use alcohol on social occasions and for relaxation. However, the abuse of alcohol through excessive drinking can interfere with good parenting. Such drinking can lead you to be inconsistent and less positive in your interactions with your child, to perceive your child's behavior as more negative than it actually is, and to use excessively harsh discipline. Furthermore, many of the behaviors you model for your child when you abuse alcohol, including the excessive drinking itself, are not ones you want your child to copy. Turning to alcohol as an escape from the problem behaviors of your strong-willed child does not work—the strong-willed behavior is still there when you sober up.

If you drink, you need to consider how this affects you as a parent. The following practices and principles will help you address the influence of your alcohol use on your child and reduce the negative effects:

- **Monitor and evaluate your drinking patterns.** When, how much, and how often do you drink? Keep a record of when you do and don't drink and what is happening during these times. This can help you identify what conditions are associated with increases and decreases in drinking and whether your drinking alcohol interferes with parenting. If it does, change your drinking patterns yourself or seek professional help.

- **Rely on your spouse's opinion about your drinking patterns.** Those who drink excessively are rarely good judges of their own drinking.
- **Work toward consistent parenting.** If you have clear guidelines for yourself as a parent, your parenting will be less influenced by your drinking.
- **Don't drink and discipline!** If you drink, do not try to discipline your child when you are under the influence of alcohol. Have your spouse or someone else assume disciplining responsibilities during this time.

Tackling Your Family's Stressors

As you can see from the topics discussed thus far, a number of factors can influence your parenting and your child's behavior. If these areas are not issues for your family, count yourself as fortunate. However, many parents do need to actively address one or more of these areas. If you are among them, first decide if a family stressor is so severe that you need professional help, and if you do, get it!

If not, then focus on the problem area you think can be solved most easily. Do not worry about any other problems—just direct all your energy and effort toward working out an acceptable solution for this one area. Once you have reached a solution, move to the next problem area and work on it. In this way, you can be focused rather than overwhelmed. Also, because you picked the easiest problem to solve first, you can enjoy your success and increase your motivation to address more difficult problems.

Screen Time

The tremendous growth in the availability of electronic media over recent years has resulted in children spending an increasing amount of time sitting in front of a screen. However, despite the growing use of computers, video games, and DVDs/videos, television remains the dominant electronic media in the lives of most young children. In fact watching television is at an all-time high for children ages two to five. Sadly, at the present time, children in the United States spend more time watching television than they do in any other activity except sleeping. It is important to understand that television can have both negative and positive effects on children. The violence, sexual activity, and alcohol and drug use often seen on television are clearly negative. Many programs imply that power, fame, and physical attractiveness are the most important personal qualities to strive for. Characters are often not held accountable for their actions, and violence is frequently used as a solution to problems. It is a developmental fact that children who are under seven years of age have a hard time telling the difference between fantasy and reality. This makes them more likely to accept the stereotypes they see and makes them vulnerable to the violence they see on television. Many experts also consider young children "defenseless" against advertising because they accept claims at face value.

In some cases, it isn't what your child is watching but what he isn't doing instead that may be most harmful. As time watching television increases, children spend less time in physical activities, reading, playing with other children, and interacting with family members. This can lead to children being overweight, less creative, less prepared to achieve academically, and less socially skilled.

Of particular importance to parents of strong-willed children are the findings that increased television viewing is related to increased aggression and lower levels of language development among young children. Since strong-willed children are already prone to behavior problems such as aggression, the added impact of television can be significant. In regard to language development, researchers recently found that for every hour the television is on, even if it is just in the background, parents spoke 500 to 1,000 fewer words to their children (and the children spoke less too). Given the importance of parent-child conversations in improving children's language skills, which in turn lead to reading skills and later academic achievement, this is extremely important.

On the other hand, it is important to realize there are some excellent television programs that promote learning and growth. Many educational programs teach important skills such as counting, spelling, and effective problem solving. Children also can learn how to interact with others positively as well as gain knowledge about various places, people, and things through television programs. The bottom line is that television programs can have a good or bad influence on children. This means that you have a tremendous responsibility in making decisions as to what your child should and should not be allowed to view. Your decisions will determine whether electronic media will have a positive or negative influence in your child's life.

Parents can do many things to minimize the negative effects of electronic media on children. At the same time, parents can encourage their children's use of electronic media as a tool for learning. Here are some suggestions:

- **Limit your child's screen time.** The American Academy of Pediatrics recommends children's total screen time should be no more than one to two hours per day of quality programming.
- **Start limiting screen time when your child is young.** If a child's screen time is limited early, he is less likely to develop a habit of excessive electronic media use as he gets older. The American Academy of Pediatrics suggests children not be allowed *any* screen time until they are two years old.

Children and Screen Time

Many people fail to realize the impact television and other forms of electronic media have on the lives of our children. Consider these facts:

- Children two to five years old spend an average of over thirty-two hours a week in front of a TV screen. Approximately twenty-five of these hours involve watching television. The remaining time is spent watching recorded media (DVDs, DVRs, videos) and/or playing video games. The thirty-two-hour total does not include time children spend using computers.
- The amount of time young children spend in front of a TV screen is steadily increasing.
- Approximately a third of children six years old or younger live in a home where the television is on most (if not all) of the time.
- It is estimated that 42 percent of four- to six-year-old children have a television in their bedroom, and 29 percent of two- to three-year-olds have a television in their bedroom.
- Only 5 to 25 percent of the average child's television viewing is of programs specifically produced for children.
- Approximately 40 percent of parents do not have rules about how much time their children under seven can spend watching television.
- By age eighteen, the average child has seen 200,000 violent acts and 16,000 murders, with 8,000 of these by the age of eleven (on television alone).
- Children ages two to seven view approximately 14,000 commercials per year on television (more than 4,400 of these are for food). Children eight to seventeen years old view 30,000 television commercials per year. Children also are increasingly being exposed to advertising on the Internet and other forms of electronic media.
- Children who watch the most television tend to have the lowest grades at school. In fact, the amount of television young children watch is a strong predictor of whether they will graduate from college.
- There is an association between young children's media exposure and later aggression as well as bullying.
- Children who read well tend to watch less television.
- More than 80 percent of households with children under twelve have broadband Internet access.
- Children two to eleven years old increased their time online by 63 percent from 2004 to 2009.

- **Set specific rules about what your child can watch.** Determine ahead of time what programs your child will be allowed to watch. Stick to your decisions!
- **Encourage viewing of age-appropriate educational programs and those with characters who are positive role models.** Encourage programs with characters who are kind, caring, and cooperative. Such programs promote positive learning.
- **Know what your child is watching.** Whenever possible, preview the programs your child wants to watch. Use a DVR or VCR to record programs for your child so that you can view them before he does.
- **Watch programs with your child.** Be available to answer his questions and provide information. This will help promote learning.
- **Do not rely on electronic media as a babysitter.** Encourage your child to entertain himself in ways other than watching television. See the recommended activities in Chapter 12 that promote imaginative and creative play.
- **Do not leave the television on in your home for "background" entertainment.** Children do not play as well with their toys when a television is on (even when it is a program they are not interested in watching). Such background television viewing has been found to be linked to less frequent, and lower quality, parent-child interactions.
- **Don't let your child eat while watching television.** Children who eat snacks or meals while watching television are more likely to overeat and become overweight.
- **Discuss violence.** If your child does view violence on television, discuss with him what he sees. Explain that often the violence seen on television is "fake." Discuss the real-life consequences for such actions. If your child sees real violence (e.g., news coverage), be available to discuss the situation at a level he can understand.
- **Get control of your own television viewing.** Set a good example. In most families, adults watch even more television than their children. Limit the amount of television that

you watch. Let your child see you reading and taking part in many activities other than watching television.

- **Do not allow your child to have a television in his bedroom.** Parents cannot effectively monitor what their child is watching on television when the television is in the bedroom. Children with a television in their bedroom spend more time watching TV than those who do not have one in their bedroom. In addition, research suggests that children who have televisions in their bedrooms have lower academic achievement.
- **Be careful in selecting video games.** Interactive video games, those involving problem-solving skills and interactions with other players, can offer advantages over more passive video games. Avoid video games that promote aggression.
- **Be knowledgeable of the rating system that is used for video games.** Only let your child play video games that are rated as appropriate for his age. Don't be hesitant to say, "No, I am not willing to buy (or rent) that game," if you have any doubts.
- **Encourage non-tech activities.** These may include reading, sports, and family activities. See Chapter 12 for suggested activities.

4

Does My Child Have ADHD?

If you haven't heard it yet, you probably will. It may be from a family member, a friend, or your child's teacher. At some point someone is probably going to say to you, "Do you think he might have ADHD?" There are few parents of strong-willed children who have not at least heard the term *attention deficit/hyperactivity disorder (ADHD)*. In recent years it has been the topic of newspaper and magazine articles, television shows, and books. The term has received so much attention that whenever a young child's behavior involves acting out and disruption, many people are quick to think that ADHD might be the cause of the problem. This chapter will help you understand more about this complex disorder, provide information to help you decide whether to seek an ADHD evaluation for your child, and if your child has the disorder, provide you with resources.

History of ADHD

Although there has been much media attention on ADHD in recent years, it is not a new disorder. In fact, professional discussion of the disorder dates back for more than a hundred years. Historians have observed that many famous and accomplished people, including Benjamin Franklin, Thomas Edison, and Albert Einstein, had behaviors consistent with ADHD.

Over the years, the disorder has had many labels, including *hyperkinesis, hyperactive child syndrome,* and *attention deficit disorder (ADD) with* or *without hyperactivity*. The fact that many different labels have been used to describe the disorder is very confusing! However, the different labels have reflected different thoughts about the disorder at different periods of time. In the 1960s, the focus was on hyperactive behavior. In the late 1970s and early 1980s, theories started focusing more on the role of attention problems; as a result, the word *attention* was incorporated into the "official" label. However, more recently, some researchers consider other issues (such as "behavioral inhibition") to play a more central role than attention. This means that the label and/or the criteria for ADHD diagnosis will probably be changed again over the next few years.

What Exactly Is ADHD?

The core symptoms of ADHD are inattention, hyperactivity, and impulsivity. It is a disorder that affects at least 3 to 7 percent of school-aged children. Boys are three times more likely to have the disorder than girls. When you hear about ADHD in the media, you may be confused by the differing estimates of how common it is. These estimates vary because the diagnostic criteria and the assessment methods used can be different across studies. Regardless of the exact percentage of children affected, ADHD is a commonly diagnosed disorder. In fact, it is estimated that on average at least one child in every classroom has ADHD. Even using conservative estimates, there are at least three million children with ADHD in the United States alone!

Russell Barkley, one of the world's leading authorities on ADHD, believes ADHD is mainly a developmental disorder of "behavioral inhibition." Simply put, children with ADHD have difficulty inhibiting (or controlling) their impulses and behavior because of neurological factors. As Dr. Barkley has pointed out in his book *Taking Charge of ADHD: The Complete, Authoritative Guide for Parents* (Guilford Press), ADHD is a very complicated disorder. It also can have a profound impact on the life of a child and his family. Children with ADHD often experience serious school difficulties and have problems in their interpersonal relationships with family members and friends. ADHD also tends to co-occur with other problems, such as learning disorders, depression, and anxiety. Of importance for you, many children with ADHD also have behavior problems similar to those of strong-willed children. These include stubbornness, not minding, and temper tantrums.

One aspect of ADHD that makes the disorder difficult to understand is that there is not one key symptom that is seen only in children with ADHD. The diagnosis is based on the frequency and intensity of specific behaviors. Of importance, the behaviors that characterize ADHD (inattention, impulsivity, and hyperactivity) occur *at least occasionally* at some level in most young children. This is not surprising, as by their very nature, many young children are often very active, impulsive, and have a short attention span. Therefore, with young children, it can be very difficult to determine whether the frequency and intensity of a child's behavior justifies a diagnosis of ADHD.

Let's look at this issue of difficulty of diagnosis a little further. Did you know that more than 50 percent of preschool-aged children are considered at some time by their parents as being inattentive or overactive? However, the vast majority of these children *do not* meet the criteria for the diagnosis of ADHD. Many children have only one or two of the behaviors associated with ADHD rather than a persistent pattern of numerous behaviors that is necessary for diagnosis. When there are only one or two behaviors of concern, preschool-aged children often will grow out of them. That is, we know that as most children increase in age, their attention span improves, they become less impulsive, and they show less overactivity. For example, research studies indicate that the vast majority of concerns about the inattentiveness or over-activity of three- to four-year-olds decreases over the course of six months without professional help. On the other hand, some young children do have the persistent pattern of behaviors required for the diagnosis of ADHD. In fact, many parents of children diagnosed with ADHD later in childhood state that they first became concerned about their child's behavior when he was three or four years old.

In the past it was believed that most children outgrew the disorder. We now know that although children may show improvements in attention, activity level, and impulsivity as they get older, many of those with ADHD often continue to have significant academic and social problems into adolescence and may even have occupational and social difficulties in adulthood. It has been estimated that 70 to 80 percent of children diagnosed with ADHD during their elementary school years will continue to display symptoms into adolescence, and 50 to 65 percent will continue to have symptoms into adulthood.

To help you better understand the core behaviors of ADHD, let's look at the primary behaviors or symptoms associated with inattention, impulsivity, and hyperactivity in a little more detail.

• **Inattention.** Problems with inattention are sometimes difficult for parents to recognize because inattention is most obvious in situations that often occur outside of the home—ones that require continued attention to activities or tasks that are boring or unexciting. In contrast, most children, even those with ADHD, can focus or pay attention when watching television or playing computer games! Problems with inattention are often more noticeable to teachers because children have to sustain their attention during detailed tasks in school. However, it is important to note that teachers may not recognize inattentive behaviors as easily as hyperactive or impulsive behaviors, which are more disruptive to the class. Specific issues related to inattention in school-aged children with ADHD may include not paying attention to details, not being able to sustain attention long enough to complete tasks, making careless mistakes, and being disorganized.

• **Impulsivity.** Children who are impulsive often do not wait for instructions to be finished before they start an activity. They tend to act before they think and, as a result, frequently do not understand what is required in a particular situation. This can lead to an ADHD child being noncompliant, as well as to a number of other difficulties. In school, these children may not do well on tests, partly because they may start answering questions before they read the test instructions. Children with ADHD also may blurt out answers to questions before a teacher or another person has finished asking the question. And because they do not wait for the full question to be asked, their answers are often wrong.

Impulsivity can also lead to other problems. Waiting in line at school and waiting for their turn in games can be very difficult. In these and other social situations, impulsive children tend to have poor physical boundaries and therefore may be seen as intrusive or bothersome by other children or adults. They also sometimes respond impulsively when they feel they have been treated unfairly, even when the other person did not intend any harm (for example, when someone accidentally steps on the child's foot). Finally, acting before thinking can lead them into dangerous situations, for example, running into the street to retrieve a ball or diving into shallow water.

• **Hyperactivity.** Children with ADHD are more active, fidgety, and restless than non-ADHD children of the same age and sex. Parents often report that their child with ADHD is "always on the go," is "on fast-forward," "talks nonstop," or "just can't sit still." These children have a hard time staying in their seats, especially at school or the dinner table.

What Causes ADHD?

The exact cause of ADHD is unclear. Since it is such a complex disorder, it is unlikely that there is a single cause. There are probably many factors that contribute to ADHD, and perhaps different factors are involved in different subtypes of ADHD.

There is a very strong genetic link to the occurrence of ADHD. In fact, the results from various studies indicate that genetic factors are the primary cause of ADHD. This means that if one member of a family has ADHD, there is a high risk for ADHD in other family members. If a parent has or has had ADHD, there is a 57 percent chance his or her child will have ADHD. If one child in a family has ADHD, there is a 32 percent chance his sibling also will have the disorder.

Current evidence indicates that several genes are involved in the transmission of ADHD. One of these genes regulates the activity of dopamine, which is a specific neurotransmitter, a chemical in the brain that carries messages from one brain cell to another. As dopamine plays a key role in initiating purposeful movement, increasing alertness, and increasing motivation, problems with this neurotransmitter would be consistent with the symptoms of ADHD. Another gene that has been implicated is one that may be related to sensation-seeking behavior in one's personality.

Another factor that can play a role in the development of ADHD for some children is injury to the brain. This includes pregnancy complications that can result from factors such as the mother's smoking or consuming alcohol during pregnancy; problems at the time of birth, such as the infant receiving insufficient oxygen; and exposure to elevated levels of toxins, such as lead, during infancy or childhood. For most children with ADHD, these types of injury are much less likely to play a role than are genetic factors.

Although our understanding of ADHD has improved in recent years, further research is needed to more fully understand this very complex disorder. Advances in technology used to study genes and the brain will be of tremendous assistance in the coming years. For example, studies have found decreased activity in several parts of the brain in children who have ADHD. And perhaps not surprisingly, some of these areas of the brain are thought to be involved in inhibiting behavior and sustaining attention.

What about other factors? Over the years, various agents such as food additives, refined sugars, and allergens have been linked to the development of ADHD. However, subsequent well-controlled studies have offered very little support for these agents as causative factors. Parenting behavior also has received attention as a possible determinant of ADHD. Although parents' behavior is important in managing behavior problems that often accompany ADHD symptoms, there is no evidence to suggest that it is a *cause* of ADHD. In short, environmental factors probably play only a minor role in determining the severity or persistence of the ADHD symptoms of inattention, impulsivity, and hyperactivity.

Should I Have My Child Evaluated?

As we discussed earlier in this chapter, many preschool-aged children may show some of the behaviors characteristic of ADHD as part of their normal development; however, relatively few children meet the diagnostic criteria for ADHD. So what should you be looking for when trying to decide if your child may have problems severe enough to be diagnosed with ADHD? The early warning signs may include a temperament that involves very high activity level, intense reactions, and moodiness. Table 4-1, "Symptoms of ADHD," lists more specific examples of the behaviors considered by professionals when determining if a child has ADHD. An important point to remember is that your child must display a significant number of these behaviors/symptoms (not just a few). It is necessary also for these problems to be longstanding *and* occur in two or more settings, for example, at home and at school. Finally, the behaviors must occur frequently *and* be clearly outside the normal range for children at a particular developmental level *and* be severe enough to cause impairments in areas such as social interactions or school functioning.

Severe cases of ADHD are relatively easy to diagnose, especially with older children. Most cases in preschool-aged children, however, as well as mild cases in older children, are

---

Symptoms of ADHD	**TABLE 4-1**

Symptoms of Inattention

- Has trouble paying attention to details; makes an abundance of careless mistakes
- Has a consistently hard time maintaining attention to activities
- Is easily distracted by things going on around him
- Doesn't appear to listen when someone is speaking to him
- Frequently does not follow directions (but not as a function of defiance or lack of understanding the directions)
- Has poor organizational skills
- Avoids activities that require paying close attention
- Frequently loses or forgets things

Symptoms of Hyperactivity

- Squirms, fidgets, and has a hard time staying in his seat
- Is very active; runs around or climbs when it is inappropriate
- Has difficulty playing quietly
- Is frequently "on the go"
- Talks nonstop

Symptoms of Impulsivity

- Blurts out answers before people finish asking questions
- Has difficulty waiting his turn in activities
- Frequently interrupts others

Adapted from the *Diagnostic and Statistical Manual of Mental Disorders*, 4th edition, Text Revision (Washington DC: American Psychiatric Association, 2000).

---

much more difficult to accurately diagnose. The line between a diagnosable disorder and the upper limits of normal behavior is not very clear. If you suspect your child might have ADHD, consult a professional for an evaluation.

If you decide to pursue a professional evaluation, it is important for you to know that there is no definitive test for ADHD. Also, professionals vary widely in how comprehensively they assess a child. Your first step should be to have your child examined by his physician to rule out other problems, such as visual or hearing difficulties. In addition, although very rare, symptoms of chronic physical problems, such as thyroid difficulties, can sometimes mimic the symptoms of

ADHD. Once such problems have been ruled out, the next step is to have a professional with expertise in assessing children with ADHD evaluate your child. This might be a psychologist, psychiatrist, pediatrician, or other professional who is trained in this area. A comprehensive evaluation typically involves interviews, behavior checklists (completed by both parents and teachers), questionnaires/tests, and sometimes observations of your child. An evaluation like this is much more likely than a brief screening, such as a short interview with you about your child's behavior, to result in an accurate diagnosis.

Treatment for ADHD

If your child is diagnosed with ADHD, you need to be aware of treatment options. First, it is critical to understand that available treatments for ADHD *do not cure* the disorder. Based on current knowledge of the disorder, it is also unlikely that a cure will be found in the near future. As a result, treatment approaches involve reducing symptoms and finding ways to more effectively manage the disorder. Thus, treatment generally needs to be ongoing over a long period of time.

Over the years there have been many fad treatments for ADHD. Most of these treatments, such as dietary changes (for example, removal of additives or sugars and use of high doses of vitamins or minerals), have not been very effective for the vast majority of children with ADHD. What we present here are more mainstream and scientifically proven treatment approaches.

The most common treatment involves the use of medication. The most effective and therefore most commonly used class of medication in managing the symptoms of ADHD is psychostimulants. This type of medication, commonly referred to simply as stimulants, includes methylphenidate-based medicines (e.g., Ritalin, Focalin, Concerta, Methylin, Metadate) and amphetamine-based medicines (Adderall, Dexedrine, DextroStat, Vyvanse). There is little doubt these medications can help many children with ADHD. However, it is important to point out that a positive response to stimulant medication does not confirm the diagnosis of ADHD. These medications would help most children, adolescents, and adults focus and become less impulsive whether they have ADHD or not. Stimulants are reported to be effective for more than 75 percent of children with ADHD. Children who don't respond to one stimulant medication may respond positively to another. Children may also respond to other nonstimulant medications such as Straterra.

Stimulant medications appear to work by boosting dopamine levels in the brain. These medications work quickly, and the effects on behavior can be observed within thirty to forty-five minutes of taking the medication (with peak effects typically within two to four hours). However, in their standard form, they typically lose their effectiveness within three to seven hours. Thus, many children must take multiple doses each day. Fortunately there are now longer-acting forms of many of these drugs that allow children to take just one pill in the morning.

Stimulant medications have their greatest impact on the symptoms of hyperactivity, impulsivity, and inattention. They also tend to improve classroom behavior and performance. However, there is currently little evidence to indicate that the use of stimulants alone results in long-term changes in any of these behaviors. That is, stimulant medications can help while they are being taken, but they do not "cure" ADHD.

Overall, stimulant medications appear to be relatively safe; however, there has been limited research on the safety of the drugs for children under five years of age. Common side effects for children of any age include sleep disturbance, decreased appetite, stomachaches, and headaches, as well as nervousness and irritability. These medications may also *slightly* slow down the growth rate of children. There is conflicting evidence as to whether this slowing rebounds after several years. The severity of most side effects is related to the dosage—the higher the dose, the more likely side effects will occur. Most of the side effects are mild and decrease over time (or with a decrease in dose). More serious side effects are rare. However, to be cautious, the American Academy of Pediatrics currently recommends that children be assessed for cardiac abnormalities before stimulant medications are prescribed. As should be the case with any medication, it is important to discuss potential side effects with a physician.

One of the critical requirements for successful treatment with medication is the use of the best dose for a given child. This often requires carefully evaluating a child's response to different doses. For this reason, it is important that the prescribing physician be experienced in the use of stimulant medications in the treatment of ADHD and that a parent and teacher carefully observe the child and keep the physician informed of his response to the medication.

As already mentioned, interventions are not limited to medication. Parents and teachers need to use effective skills to manage the oppositional behavior problems often seen in children with ADHD. These skills, which include those described in Part II of this book (our five-week program for parents of young strong-willed children), can be very helpful in reducing some of these behavior problems (for example, the oppositional behaviors not minding and temper tantrums). In contrast, individual therapy (in which a therapist spends one-on-one time with the child) has not been proven to be an effective intervention for these types of problems with young children.

Often, the best treatment approach includes both medication and use of effective behavior management skills by parents and teachers. With such a combined treatment approach, the medication primarily reduces problems with inattention, impulsivity, and hyperactivity, and the effective skills used by parents and teachers primarily address related problems such as oppositional and aggressive behavior. An alternative approach preferred by some parents and professionals for preschool-aged children is to implement the behavioral approach first. If this is not effective by itself in controlling the child's problems, then they use the combined approach.

Resources for Support and Information if Your Child Has ADHD

Children and Adults with Attention Deficit/Hyperactivity Disorder (CHADD) is a national, nonprofit organization representing children and adults with ADHD. Founded in 1987 by a group of concerned parents, the organization has grown to include more than 16,000 members and more than two hundred chapters across the United States. CHADD's goal is to improve the lives of people with ADHD through education, advocacy, and support efforts. CHADD produces several publications, including a magazine and fact sheets. The organization also holds an annual conference and maintains a website with a wealth of information (chadd.org). You may contact CHADD's national headquarters at 8181 Professional Place, Suite 150, Landover, Maryland 20785; by telephone, (301) 306-7070 or (800) 233-4050; or by submitting an online request for information at help4adhd.org/info_request.cfm.

Obtaining Special Services in School for a Child with ADHD

When a child has difficulty in the classroom because of his ADHD (e.g., if he has difficulty paying attention or finishing his work), a parent may request the school district to evaluate the child. That evaluation can help determine what special services the child would be eligible to receive at school. A parent can speak with the principal, or the director of special education in the school district, about how to formally request the evaluation. The parent may need to write a letter requesting the child be evaluated. The school district will then determine whether the child is eligible for a formal evaluation. If the evaluation is conducted, the results will determine if the child is eligible for an *individualized education plan (IEP)*. An IEP outlines the special education services the child will receive.

Children with ADHD are not automatically eligible for special education services or an IEP. However, they can be classified as *other health impaired* under the Individuals with Disabilities Education Improvement Act (IDEIA) if their ADHD "adversely affects" their educational performance. What if a child with ADHD is not found to be eligible for an IEP under IDEIA? Fortunately, he may still be eligible for classroom modifications/accommodations (e.g., modifications to work assignments, extra assistance) under Section 504 of the Rehabilitation Act. However, it is the parent who often has to pursue these services for her child.

Before pursuing special services through your child's school, we recommend you educate yourself about IDEIA and Section 504. Information is available through numerous websites including the U.S. Department of Education's website (ed.gov). By being informed, and knowing your rights, you can be a stronger advocate for your child within the school system. This will help ensure that your child obtains services, for which he is eligible, to help him to succeed in school.

PART II

Addressing Strong-Willed Behavior: A Five-Week Program

At this point, you should better understand the various factors that contribute to your strong-willed child's behavior. This understanding can help you appreciate the next dimension of our strategy: learning parenting techniques to address problems associated with your child's strong-willed behavior. The chapters in Part II teach those techniques in the form of a five-week program.

Part II starts with a discussion about how you can decide whether your child's behavior needs to change (Chapter 5). We then present our five-week program. Each of the subsequent five chapters discusses a different skill, and you learn one skill per week. The skills build on each other, so it is important that you master each skill before moving to the next. Mastery of a skill involves more than simply understanding the skill and knowing what to do. It means actually using the skill on a daily basis with your child. The skills you will be learning are attending (Chapter 6), rewarding (Chapter 7), ignoring (Chapter 8), giving your child effective instructions (Chapter 9), and using time-outs correctly (Chapter 10). Each of these skills has been shown in our research and research conducted by others to be important for improving the behavior of strong-willed children. However, as we discuss in Chapter 11, it is the integration of these skills that leads to maximum effectiveness in changing your child's behavior.

5

Does My Child's Behavior Really Need to Change?

"I have to tell Karen to pick up her toys at least ten times before she does it!"

"Jimmy stamps his foot and yells 'no' when I tell him to take a bath."

"Amanda is a terror in the grocery store—always demanding candy, running up and down the aisles, grabbing things, and throwing tantrums."

"At supper Bob constantly picks at his sister. He mimics her, kicks her under the table, and interrupts her every time she tries to say something."

"Tracy seems to know that when I am on the phone, she can do whatever she wants to do and I can't do anything about it."

"If I want Greg to do anything, I have to tell him at least five times before he will do it."

Do these statements sound like ones you make about your child? If so, using the five-week program presented in the following chapters will decrease the problem behaviors of your strong-willed child and improve the relationship between the

| **Problem Behaviors of Strong-Willed Children** | **WORKSHEET 5-1** |

Which of the following words and phrases describe your child or his behavior? Place a check in the box in front of each behavior your child engages in at least occasionally. If your child shows many of these behaviors, the five-week program should be particularly helpful.

☐ Is disobedient   ☐ Is irritable

☐ Has temper tantrums   ☐ Swears

☐ Demands attention   ☐ Is aggressive

☐ Is stubborn   ☐ Blames others

☐ Screams   ☐ Is sassy

☐ Argues   ☐ Is destructive

☐ Threatens others   ☐ Lies

☐ Shows off   ☐ Is negative

two of you. The skills you will learn are ones all parents should use. However, the program was originally developed and shown to be clinically effective with strong-willed children who have high rates of noncompliant and other disruptive behaviors. This chapter focuses on deciding whether you and your child need this program.

Problem Behaviors

One way to decide whether you need the five-week program is to evaluate whether your child often engages in types of behaviors that are problematic. Worksheet 5-1 lists more than a dozen problem behaviors—mainly the noncompliant and disruptive behaviors common among strong-willed children. While several of the behaviors listed on the worksheet, such as temper tantrums and stubbornness, are very common among strong-willed children, other behaviors such as lying and swearing occur less frequently. However, these more "severe" behavior problems can develop if the more common behavior problems associated with being strong-willed are not handled effectively and are allowed to escalate over time. If your child shows many of these behaviors, the five-week program should be particularly beneficial.

Problem Situations

Another way to evaluate whether your strong-willed child's behavior warrants the five-week program is to consider how he behaves in situations that often present problems. To help you do this, Worksheet 5-2 lists a number of common situations in which parents frequently interact with two- to six-year-old children. These situations focus on routine activities such as going to bed at night, taking a bath, and grocery shopping.

In the first column next to each situation, indicate whether your child's behavior is a problem in that situation. Do you have difficulty with your child complying with your instructions in each situation? In the next column, note how often your child is a problem in this situation. For example, think about putting your child to bed at night. Is it difficult getting your child to go to bed every night of the week or perhaps only one or two nights out of the week?

In the next two columns, write down what typically happens in each problem situation. What do you do? What does your child do? Returning to the bedtime example, do you tuck your child in bed and tell him "good night" but find he gets out of bed and comes into the room where you are watching television? If so, what do you then do? Do you put him back in bed or let him stay up? If you put him back to bed, does he get up again? If so, what do you do then?

For each problem situation, list what your child does and what you do in response. Of particular importance is what happens at the end of the interaction between you and your child. In the bedtime example, do you eventually give up and let your child stay up?

Situations in Which Strong-Willed Children Often Display Problems

Situation	Is There a Problem?	How Often?	What Do You Do?	What Does Your Child Do?
Going to bed				
Getting up in the morning				
Mealtime				
Bath time				
When you are on the phone				
When you have visitors at home				
Riding in the car				
Grocery shopping				
Eating in restaurants				

Many parents have found completing this worksheet to be an eye-opening experience. They discover that most of these routine situations involve problems with their child's behavior. That was true of the mother whose words, following, tell what happens when she is on the phone:

> *The minute I get on the phone with my mother or a friend, it's like Steve's antenna goes up and he realizes he can get away with anything. He torments his sister, jumps on the sofa, crawls up on the kitchen counter to grab candy, and starts throwing things out of the refrigerator. It's incredible, and I'm trapped in a conversation and can only helplessly watch him and become more and more frustrated. I now dread the phone ringing!*

Some parents experience problems with their child in only one or two of the situations presented in Worksheet 5-2. If you are one of these parents, spending five weeks in the parenting program is one way—and a very good way—to solve these problems and improve your overall relationship with your child. However, most parents we have worked with experience problems with their child in many of the situations. This behavior pattern suggests problems in the general interactions between parent and child. Under these circumstances, it is very important to use the five-week program to change these general interactions rather than trying to solve each problem situation individually. Improving the general interactions solves many of the individual problems with a strong-willed child because the child becomes more cooperative overall and thus more willing to do what the parent requests. At the same time, the parent gains a general set of skills to use with different problem situations that may arise. In other words, the five-week program will help you acquire skills to be a problem solver in a variety of difficult situations with your strong-willed child.

Degree of Compliance

Another way to determine the magnitude of your child's problem behaviors is to set up a structured interaction with him. This will give you some firsthand information about the difficulties between you and your child. All you need for this interaction is a few toys and some time alone with your child. You give your child a series of instructions and see if he complies with your requests. Strong-willed children typically are not very compliant!

Mark Roberts, a psychologist at Idaho State University, has developed a standard set of thirty instructions, called the *Compliance Test*, that parents can use to examine how compliant their child is. The first ten of the thirty instructions are presented in Table 5-1. To administer this test, tell your child that you want him to do some things for you. Lay out the toys described in the instructions in Table 5-1, then issue the instructions exactly as they are presented. Do not say or do anything else. This may be difficult and feel uncomfortable, as you probably are used to giving your child reasons for why you are telling him to do things. However, by only giving instructions, you will have a clear picture of how he responds to your directions. Issuing just the ten instructions in the table should be sufficient for you to know how compliant your child is. Furthermore, based on recent research by Robert J. McMahon and his colleagues, some children become distressed when all thirty instructions are given.

Record whether or not your child complies within five seconds, then issue the next instruction. Continue until you have issued all ten instructions. You probably will observe several things as you issue the instructions. First, your child may comply less often as you issue more instructions. This is common, so don't be surprised. Second, very few children comply with all of the instructions. Therefore, you should not expect perfect compliance; it is neither realistic nor desirable.

How do you know if your child has a problem with compliance? If he complies less than 60 percent of the time (six of the ten instructions), you will have reason to question how

| **Compliance Test Instructions** | **TABLE 5-1** |

Toys needed: cat, bear, dog, frog, box,
two cars, dump truck, rabbit, person, two blocks.
(Note: Substitutions with other toys are acceptable.)

1. Put the cat in the box.

2. Put the bear in the box.

3. Put the frog in the box.

4. Put the dog in the box.

5. Put the rabbit in the box.

6. Put this block in the truck.

7. Put this car in the truck.

8. Put the person in the truck.

9. Put this block in the truck.

10. Put this animal in the truck.

Source: Mark W. Roberts, professor of psychology, Idaho State University.
Reprinted with permission.

compliant he is. However, you should consider other factors as well. For example, does he talk back to you ("You can't make me do it"), become aggressive, or sulk? All of these behaviors, as well as his actual compliance, should provide you with valuable information about your child's behavior and the extent to which he is strong-willed. Not surprisingly, parents whose children score low on the Compliance Test have reports such as the following about their child's routine behavior:

> *It's so frustrating! I can't get Mark to bed at night, and then I can't get him up in the morning. I tell him to get up, I shake him, I keep going back into his room, but he just will not get up. I finally sit him up in bed and dress him while he screams and pouts. By then we are both foul and it is so late that breakfast is horrible and rushed. Who would have ever thought that we would start out almost every day this way!*

> *Tracy is amazing—she never wants to take a bath, but once she gets in the tub, I can't get her out! As*

soon as I say that it's bath time, she screams and runs. I have to literally fight with her to undress her and then almost drag her to the tub. Once she is in the water, she's fine until it's time to get out. The fight then starts all over again! I have to drag her out kicking and screaming and try to dry off and dress an irritable child who cries and acts like she's dying!

Let's look for a moment at why we focus on child compliance and noncompliance. Several clinical researchers have suggested that noncompliance is the cornerstone of behavior problems for young children. What does this mean? First, noncompliance is the most frequently occurring behavior problem among young children. Second, and perhaps even more important, noncompliance is the problem behavior that sets the stage for other problem behaviors. That is, if noncompliance is not a problem early on, a child is unlikely to engage in behaviors that may be problems in the preschool years or even later on. These other problem behaviors build upon the original behavior of noncompliance. Thus, it is important to determine if noncompliance is a primary problem behavior of your child—which is likely among strong-willed children.

Let's return to the situations in Worksheet 5-2. Is your child noncompliant in most of these situations? For example, does he fail to comply when you instruct him to go to bed, come to the dinner table, or get out of the bathtub? Each of these situations represents a time when you are trying to have your child comply with instructions. Furthermore, in both the daily situations (Worksheet 5-2) and the Compliance Test (Table 5-1), your child may demonstrate some of the problem behaviors listed in Worksheet 5-1, "Problem Behaviors of Strong-Willed Children." For example, he may argue, scream, and become aggressive. As you probably are beginning to see, all of the information about your child's behavior that you've gathered from the observations and exercises in this chapter fit together to form a picture of a strong-willed child.

Your Frustration Level

There is one final test for whether you should undertake the five-week program. This one is very easy and requires only a few minutes of careful thought. Answer this one question: am I often frustrated by my child's behavior and by my failure to help my child behave better? If the answer is "yes," you are a parent who wants something better for your child and for yourself. The five-week parenting program is for you!

Introduction to the Five-Week Program

The five-week program for addressing strong-willed behavior consists of five parenting skills to be learned one skill at a time. The skills build on one another, so it is important to master the first skill before moving to the next. Mastering a skill involves more than simply understanding the skill and knowing what to do; you must actually use the skill on a daily basis with your child. That is why you learn only one skill per week. Believe it or not, it takes at least a week to master a new parenting skill and make it part of your daily routine!

Thus, in each week of the five-week program you will be introduced to a skill and then practice that skill daily over the course of a week. Once you have mastered the skill, which should require a week but could well take longer, you move on to the next skill. However, you do *not* move on until you have mastered the skill. This is the strength of the program—it involves actual behavior change on the part of you and your child. So, you should practice each skill repeatedly until it is part of your everyday routine with your child.

It is far more effective if *both* mother and father in two-parent homes undertake the five-week program. If both of you go through the program together, you can expect greater improvement in your child's behavior as well as improved relationships among all family members. Furthermore, if both of you participate, you can practice skills with each other before you try them with your child. One parent can play the role of the child, and the other parent can play the role of the parent. One parent practices the skills, and then the roles are reversed. This might be uncomfortable at first, but it can help you learn the skill so that you use it consistently and effectively with your child.

The Smith and Jones Families

To help you see the types of problems experienced by other families with a strong-willed child and how the five-week program can help, let's look at two hypothetical families. We'll call them the Smiths and the Joneses, and we will follow both families throughout the five-week program.

The Smith Family

John and Barbara Smith grew up together in a small town in the Midwest. After John completed a trade school, they married and moved to a city in a neighboring state so John could take a job in sales with a young but growing company.

Almost immediately after the move, to the delight of both Barbara and John, Barbara became pregnant. Nine months later Susan was born. During the next two years, Barbara devoted herself to being a homemaker and caring for Susan. John worked long hours, but everyone who knew him could tell that his family was an important priority.

Shortly after Susan's second birthday, again to the delight of both of the Smiths, Barbara became pregnant again. Nine months later Tim was born. Almost immediately Barbara and John noted that Tim was a very different baby than Susan had been. Whereas Susan would lie in her bed cooing or play contentedly on the floor, Tim often was cranky, slept poorly at night, and was difficult to feed, as he would take small amounts of milk and then cry and spit it up. When Susan was an infant, Barbara would cheerfully greet John at the door when he returned home from work. At the same stage of Tim's life, she often was irritated, tired, and frustrated when John arrived home. John's evenings changed from relaxing, casually playing with his daughter, recounting his day in detail, and listening to Susan to assuming many of the responsibilities with Tim in the evening. Throughout the night John and Barbara would alternate who would respond to Tim's crying, which occurred every two to three hours.

Over the next two years, Tim's behavior changed, but unfortunately, it did not improve. Instead of crying to be picked up, Tim was crawling and walking around the house destroying magazines, framed pictures, and his sister's dolls. Barbara found herself becoming the "No" Mommy. In her own words, "It seemed like every time I had something to say to Tim, it began with 'No, don't do that, Tim.'" Barbara found herself spanking Tim more and more, creating excuses to leave the house as soon as John came home, and having recurring thoughts along the lines of "I love Tim, but I sure do not like him!" These thoughts usually were followed by feelings of guilt, especially when Tim was asleep at night.

As Tim grew older, his behavior problems appeared to accelerate. It seemed that he was constantly picking at his sister; screaming, "You can't make me do it!" at his mother; refusing to comply with even the simplest instruction from either parent; and taking hours to go to sleep at night. His behavior outside the home with his parents was no better. In the grocery store, Tim would break away from his mother and run through the aisles. When Barbara would catch up with him, he would immediately start screaming, fall down on the floor, and have a full-blown tantrum. Barbara simply could not handle him in public places. As a result, all trips outside the home with Tim were limited to times when his father could be present. In fact, all trips outside the home were limited to those that were absolutely necessary!

Beyond their concerns with their two children, Barbara and John were not doing so well themselves. Barbara was frequently moody and depressed, whereas John worked longer hours and was more irritable during the time that he did spend at home. He often snapped at Barbara, and he spent less and less time with both of the children. He fussed about how disorganized the house was, saying, "I can't deal with all my work stress and the mess at home."

During this time, Barbara and John finally came to the realization that Tim's strong-willed behavior was a problem that they must address. Furthermore, Barbara and John realized that their home environment and their relationship were not very positive. Playing with the children, having family talks around the kitchen table, watching television together, and enjoying picnics as a family in the park just were not occurring anymore. The fun times were gone, and family life had become a chore. As a result, John and Barbara decided to make a joint concerted effort to improve Tim's behavior and make their home a more positive place for everyone. Just making that decision raised their spirits and their enthusiasm for their family.

The Jones Family

Ed and Patricia Jones met during their third year of college, when they were in the same journalism class at a state university on the East Coast. Although they had very different interests, each was attracted to the other. Ed enjoyed sports, parties, and large groups of friends. In contrast, Patricia enjoyed watching movies at home and romantic dinners. Nevertheless, Ed and Patricia were head over heels in love, and as soon as they completed college, they married.

Ed and Patricia moved to a large city on the West Coast, where Ed took a position with a large firm and Patricia became a freelance writer. She became successful almost immediately when several of her articles were published in popular magazines. In fact, her success appeared to put a distance between Ed and her, as he received little recognition and no promotions in his firm.

When Patricia became pregnant at twenty-nine, it appeared to improve her relationship with Ed. For the first time in several years, they had a common goal: raising a child. When Lisa was born, Patricia and Ed assumed the role of doting parents. Perhaps surprisingly, Lisa responded positively to her parents' excessive attention and was viewed by everyone as a sweet child.

Patricia's life revolved around Lisa and her continuing success as a freelance writer. Feeling excluded from the relationship between Lisa and her mother, as well as unable to share Patricia's career success, Ed distanced himself from the family. He soon returned to activities he had enjoyed before marriage, spending his extra time at sporting events and local bars.

Patricia and Ed began to quarrel more frequently about his behavior. At first these quarrels occurred when Lisa was asleep; however, they soon began to spill over into the rest of the day and would occur in front of her. Finally, Ed and Patricia agreed to separate. Eventually, they divorced. Lisa was now four and a half years old.

The divorce was not easy for any of the Joneses. Ed appeared to be even less interested in Lisa than he had been, and Patricia became more involved in her work and entered a new romantic relationship. However, no one changed more than Lisa; she was no longer viewed as a sweet child but rather as a strong-willed child. Once Lisa decided to do something, there was nothing that Patricia could do to change her mind. Furthermore, she typically refused to do even the simplest activities that enable a single parent and child to get through a typical day. Lisa refused to put on her coat in the morning when leaving for preschool, refused to get out of the car when they arrived at the preschool, refused to take a bath, and interrupted her mother constantly with questions and demands whenever Patricia was on the telephone. Patricia found herself coaxing, pleading, demanding, threatening, and, at times, screaming at Lisa—none of which worked.

At first Patricia thought Lisa's behavior would settle down with time. However, after six months, Patricia realized Lisa's behavior was becoming worse, not better. Patricia knew that she needed to do more than wait for Lisa to "grow out of" her bad behavior. She needed help!

We will be returning to these families in subsequent chapters as they learn the skills in our five-week program.

6

Week 1: Attending

The first skill in the five-week parenting program is *attending*—describing your child's appropriate behavior and, at times, imitating what your child is doing. In many ways, it is one of the most important skills because it lays the groundwork for a more positive relationship between you and your child. Building on this relationship, you can learn the remaining skills more effectively, and your child's behavior will improve more quickly and to a greater extent. Attending is really very simple. It allows you to tune in to your child's behavior and lets your child know that you are very interested in the positive things he does. If you think about your strong-willed child's behavior, many of your thoughts may focus on the negative aspects. Attending will give you a chance to reverse this situation by noticing some of his positive behaviors.

It is important for you to know before beginning the program that our research indicates many parents find attending to be one of the most difficult skills to learn. That is because the negative aspects of your strong-willed child's behavior are what is most evident to you. As a result, to learn and use attending with your child's positive behaviors will require substantial effort on your part. However, our research also suggests that parents who learn and use attending report that it is a very useful skill. And, research summarized across many studies on teaching effective parenting skills indicates the attending skill is a critical one for increasing appropriate behavior of young children.

To see how important attending to your child's positive behaviors can be, think about bosses for whom you have worked. How did they relate to you and other employees? Try to think of the top three characteristics of the supervisor for whom you *most* enjoyed working and the top three characteristics of the supervisor for whom you *least* enjoyed working. When people list such characteristics, they often come up with surprisingly similar answers. Characteristics of the supervisors they least enjoyed working for include being overly negative, taking their employees for granted, and not being understanding. The supervisors people most enjoyed working for are often described as being appreciative of employees' work, being understanding and warm, and providing employees with a lot of positive feedback. Research shows that employees whose supervisors provide positive feedback are not only happier in their jobs but also more productive. Your role in the parent-child relationship is much like that of a supervisor.

When you think about your relationship with your child, how would you describe your characteristics as his "supervisor"? Many parents of strong-willed children fall into a cycle in which they become overly negative and provide less than optimal levels of warmth and positive feedback. Strong-willed children may perceive, often accurately, that their parents always notice their inappropriate behavior but rarely notice or acknowledge their appropriate behavior. So they continue to behave inappropriately, and their parents become more and more negative. In contrast, parents who learn and use the attending skill are perceived as warmer and more aware of a child's appropriate behavior. Through the use of attending skills, parents improve the way they relate to their children, which can result in their child's becoming not only more contented but also more willing to cooperate.

The Role of Attending

When parents use the attending skill, it communicates that they do notice and are interested in their child's appropriate behavior. If a positive family life exists (see Chapter 12), a child will value his parents' attention. Under these conditions, attending to your child's appropriate behavior will increase the likelihood that he will behave appropriately more of the time.

Here are some examples of how a parent attends to a child's behavior:

- "My, you're stacking the blocks high!"
- "You're putting the yellow block on top of the blue block!"
- "Now you're driving the truck!"
- "You're turning the truck around in a circle!"
- "You're coloring the picture red!"
- "You're coloring the sky blue!"
- "You're lining up all the toys!"
- "You're putting the ball next to the bucket!"
- "You're blowing up the balloon!"
- "The balloon is getting so big!"
- "Whoops, the balloon broke!"

Notice that the parent gives no instructions and asks no questions. The parent simply describes exactly what the child is doing. Also notice that there is an exclamation point after each statement. This means that the attending statements are said with positive emotion and enthusiasm. It is not only what you say that is important but how you say it!

Beyond describing, a parent also may be imitating what her child is doing. For example, if he is stacking blocks, the parent may also stack blocks. Imitation not only communicates approval of the child's behavior but also teaches young children how to play with others.

Attending sounds simple. However, as we already have noted, it isn't! Most parents of strong-willed children do not

Two Styles of Interacting

Here are two transcripts of interactions between a parent and a child. In the first interaction, the parent mainly gives instructions and asks questions. In the second interaction, the parent uses only attending. Each statement is marked with an (i) for an instruction, a (q) for a question, or an (a) for an attend.

Interaction Dominated by Instructions and Questions

Parent: Let's play now. (i)
Child: OK.
Parent: What do you want to play? (q)
Child: I don't know.
Parent: Well, we don't have long. Decide now. (i)
Child: Let's play blocks.
Parent: That will be fun.
Child: I know.
Parent: Move them over here so we can play. (i)
Child: OK.
Parent: Why don't you make a castle? (q)
Child: OK.
Parent: You are really stacking the blocks high. (a)
Child: I know.
Parent: So, do you think you can make a castle like in the picture? (q)
Child: I don't know.
Parent: Well, try to make one. (i)
Child: I will.
Parent: Then you should put the big blocks on the bottom. (i)

Interaction Dominated by Attends

Parent: You're ready to play now! (a)
Child: I sure am.
Parent: Yesterday you built a big fort.
Child: Yes! Today I'm going to build a castle.
Parent: That will be great!
Child: Yeah.
Parent: Now you're putting the brown blocks in a big circle! (a)
Child: They will be my moat.

Parent: Boy, you sure can build high walls! (a)
Child: Now I'm going to build a tower.
Parent: Wow, you're making it so tall. (a)
Child: I hope it doesn't fall down.
Parent: You're putting up some neat buildings inside the castle. (a)
Child: Yeah, they're for the soldiers to sleep in.
Parent: And now you put in a gate! (a)
Child: The king and all his men need a gate to get in.

The differences may appear subtle, but this parent is communicating two very different messages to her child. In the first dialogue, the parent is communicating that she is in charge and that her agenda, not the child's, is more important. In the second dialogue, the parent is communicating that she is interested in her child and his activities.

spend much time just paying attention to their child's appropriate behavior. Rather, their interactions primarily involve instructions and questions. Such an interaction style indicates that parents of a strong-willed child typically are interested in having their child respond to them by behaving as directed or answering questions. Many parents interact with their strong-willed child almost exclusively by using instructions and questions. In addition, these parents often fail to follow up on the instructions by making sure their child complies or to follow up on the questions by waiting for an answer. As a result, a strong-willed child tends to tune his parents out and, over time, complies with instructions and responds to questions less and less often. Unfortunately, the more a child tunes out his parents, the more instructions and questions parents feel they need to issue in order to try to gain compliance just once in a while. As you can see, a vicious circle begins: the less a child responds, the more instructions and questions a parent issues; the more instructions and questions a parent issues, the less the child responds!

To improve interactions with your strong-willed child, you must change this negative cycle of issuing many instructions and questions and rarely receiving compliance or answers. Using attending is the first step. The objective of this chapter is for you to learn the skill and, later in the week, begin applying it to your daily interactions with your child.

The Smith and Jones Families

Let's observe how the Smith and Jones families learned to incorporate attending into their daily lives.

The Smith Family

John and Barbara Smith were concerned about Tim's strong-willed behavior. They had decided to try making changes in his behavior and in their family life. One of these changes was to become more positive with Tim, and both of the Smiths realized that attending was an excellent way to do this. Barbara and John read about attending skills. Initially, John felt that describing Tim's behavior over and over sounded rather silly. However, he agreed to practice attending with Barbara so they could both learn how to use the skill.

The attending skills were harder for Barbara and John to learn than they first expected. Both parents caught themselves asking questions ("What are you doing?") and telling Tim what to do, rather than simply describing his activity during playtimes. At first Barbara, who was with Tim more than John, was more committed to her practice sessions with their son and was able to set aside designated playtimes to spend with him every day. However, John was more than willing to observe Barbara practicing with Tim. At these times he noticed how many questions and instructions she used in the interaction. This made him think about his own behavior with Tim. He began to realize that at the dinner table, during bath time, and when playing ball outside, almost everything he said to his son was a question or an instruction to do something.

As John observed more of the play sessions between Barbara and Tim, he also realized that as Barbara's behavior became more positive and attentive and less demanding and questioning, Tim appeared to enjoy his mother's company more and played in a less rambunctious and more cooperative manner. Watching Barbara and Tim led John to conclude, "Maybe there is something to this attending business." At the same time, Barbara was having a similar reaction to her own experiences in using the attending skills with Tim and her observations of John and Tim in their increasingly frequent play sessions.

Barbara and John began discussing ways to use attending at times other than during designated playtimes with Tim and also to use the skills with his older sister, Susan. Barbara found that if she brought Tim's toys into the kitchen, he would play on the floor with them while she described his activities and cooked dinner. Susan also was responsive to Barbara's attending. In fact, she would grin at her mother and say, "I like being with you, Mommy." John began using attending skills when he and Tim went grocery shopping. Instead of listening to the radio while in the car, John turned it off and described the scenery along the roadside to Tim; he also described his son's behavior. Tim's behavior changed almost immediately from constant squirming and trying to get out of his seat belt to listening and talking with his father.

John and Barbara began to realize that attending was exactly the opposite of what they had been doing. In the past, when Tim was acting up, they would usually attend to him, most of the time in a negative way. Whenever he was behaving appropriately, they had been adhering to the philosophy "Let sleeping dogs [or children] lie." John said, "Tim was good so seldom that whenever he was good, we weren't going to say anything because he might quit being good."

Barbara and John realized that the attending skill was designed to tune them in to Tim's good behavior. The more they did this, the more they realized that Tim was not always bad, and they actually enjoyed being with him, at least some of the time. For his part, Tim seemed to enjoy and respond well to the attention, thus allowing extended positive interactions to occur with his parents. There were still many difficult times, and Tim continued to be strong-willed when it came to complying with his parents' instructions. However, at least they had made a start. Something positive was happening in the Smith family.

The Jones Family

Patricia Jones was having increasing problems with Lisa's strong-willed behavior after she and Ed divorced. Attending was particularly difficult for Patricia, largely because as a single mom she could not find designated time periods to practice the attending skills with Lisa. She had not realized the amount of time and effort required to become more child-focused. After all, her life was busy, and Ed had transferred to the East Coast for a long-awaited promotion. Although they never discussed it, both of the Joneses knew that raising Lisa was Patricia's responsibility.

Patricia knew that she had to practice the attending skills in order to master them and help change Lisa's behavior. She soon realized that extra time to practice the skill was not necessary. Instead, she began having practice sessions at times when she was already with Lisa. She practiced attending with her daughter in the car while going to and from Lisa's day care center, and she practiced the skills at night when she and Lisa ate dinner together. At first, Lisa was not too enthusiastic about this because it involved turning off the TV so that she and her mother could focus on each other. However, as her mother's attention increased, Lisa's insistence on watching TV diminished and finally dropped out altogether.

Lisa's behavior began to become less difficult. Lisa and Patricia enjoyed more positive times together, such as lying on the bed and giggling and laughing together. Patricia found that she was enjoying her time with Lisa more and more. Lisa still demanded attention and wanted to do things her own way, but the good times seemed to be occurring more and more often.

Learning to Attend

The most effective way to learn attending skills is to set aside specific practice sessions. During these practice sessions, the parent describes aloud what the child is doing. When a parent is attending well during a practice session, anyone overhearing should be able to tell exactly what the child is doing. Attending is very similar to a sportscaster giving play-by-play commentary on a sporting event. During initial practice sessions, many parents feel uncomfortable and almost silly using the attending skill because it makes them sound childlike. In fact, this is exactly how we want you to sound!

To get started with your practice sessions, set aside at least two ten-minute periods per day. These are times when you and your child can sit down in a play situation without being interrupted. Finding such practice times is difficult for today's busy families. However, it is *absolutely necessary* that you set aside times if you are going to effectively learn the attending skill; this is also true for learning the other skills. To improve your strong-willed child's behavior, you have to make both the quantity and quality of time you spend with your child a high priority so you can learn the skills effectively. We call this becoming *child-focused*. When you are child-focused, all of your attention, thoughts, and verbalization are focused on your child. You are not thinking about dinner, work, or anything else. Just your child!

Once you complete the program, you will be able to decrease some of your focus on your child; however, you may not want to give up this special time with him. You may find being with your child is much more pleasant and rewarding than it ever was!

Within each ten-minute practice session, sit down on the floor with your child and have a number of toys available for play. Tell your child that you want to play whatever he wants to play (within reason). During the playtime, your job is to describe your child's appropriate behavior with attending statements. If he displays minor inappropriate behavior during the practice session, try to ignore it. Besides attending to appropriate behavior, you also may imitate your child's play behavior, but in doing so, you should not guide or structure his activities. Like describing, imitation says, "I am interested in you and what you are doing." Of equal importance, you should not use instructions and questions or try to teach your child during the practice sessions, for example, "Johnny, this block is red." This is your child's time to direct the activity.

If you are like many parents of strong-willed children, you may be so accustomed to giving instructions and asking questions that you are not even aware of how much you are interacting with your child in this way. As a result, it can be very helpful to tape-record your practice time with your child and listen to it later. Or you can have your spouse or someone else note the number of attends, instructions, and questions you give in the practice session. In either case, you may be surprised at how many instructions and questions you issue.

When parents begin trying to use fewer instructions and questions during these play interactions with their child, they often have a hard time thinking of how to turn what they instinctively want to say into attending. In the practice situation, you need to carefully think about each statement you are about to make. Thus, if you think about saying "Are you stacking the blocks?" you can change the question into an attending statement by simply saying, "Now you're stacking the blocks!" Such a statement demands nothing of your child but lets him know that you are interested in his activities.

Sometimes a child will say something like "Why are you talking funny?" or "Why are you saying those things?" You can say, "I am just interested in how you are playing." Most of the time this will be enough of an explanation. If your child continues to question you, ignore the questions and focus on attending with interest and enthusiasm. If your child appears to become overstimulated, you can reduce your rate of attends. But remember, this is mainly a practice session for you to learn the attending skills.

Continue the two ten-minute practice sessions with your child for seven days. (Sorry, but there are no weekends or holidays for parents!) After each practice session, listen to the tape recording of the session or receive feedback from the person who observed the session. You want to be giving at least

Guidelines for Practice Sessions: Attending	**TABLE 6-1**

Do Not	**Do**
Issue any instructions	Attend to (describe) your child's appropriate behavior
Ask any questions	
Try to teach	Imitate your child's play behavior
	Tape-record the session or have someone observe the session
	Evaluate your performance
	Reward yourself for your efforts and performance
	Recognize that learning to attend effectively will require substantial work on your part

four attends per minute (forty in a ten-minute practice session!) and no more than four instructions plus questions during the entire ten minutes. What is particularly important is that you, just as you do with your child, focus on the positive parts of your performance. Do not be overly critical; you are learning a new approach to parenting, and it will take time. Reward yourself for taking the time, putting forth the effort, and improving your performance as a parent. Pat yourself on the back, compliment yourself, take a leisurely stroll, watch your favorite television comedy show—do something really pleasant and reinforcing for yourself. Parenting is hard work, and your efforts should be rewarded!

The guidelines for the attending practice sessions are summarized in Table 6-1.

Take a look at Worksheet 6-1 and note that after Day 3, you will need to take on a second assignment. Find two "natural times" during the day to use attending with your child for at least five minutes each. This might be while you are riding in the car with your child, sitting with him while he takes a bath, or grocery shopping together. All of these, as well as many other daily interactions with your child, are excellent times to begin incorporating the attending skill into your

Daily Assignments for Week 1: Attending	***WORKSHEET 6-1***						
	Days						
Tasks	1	2	3	4	5	6	7
1. Two ten-minute practice times	☐	☐	☐	☐	☐	☐	☐
2. Two five-minute natural times				☐	☐	☐	☐
3. Thirty-minute period: fifteen attends					☐	☐	☐

daily routine. It is only when the skill becomes a natural part of your daily interactions with your strong-willed child that his behavior and your relationship with him will begin to improve.

Finally, after Day 4 and continuing for the rest of the week, pick a half-hour period when you and your child are both at home together. This may be late in the afternoon or during the evening after dinner. Your job is to give your child at least fifteen attends during this half hour. Some parents have bought a golf wrist-counter in order to keep up with how many attends they give and to remind themselves that they are supposed to be attending during these practice times. These parents have reported that wearing the counter really helped them remember to provide frequent attends. If you prefer, substitute another reminder, such as a rubber band on your wrist.

Worksheet 6-1 outlines the daily requirements for you this week in terms of learning and using the attending skill. Use the checkboxes provided in the worksheet to check off when you have completed each day's assignment.

Practicing Your New Skill

You may be thinking, "Should I never issue another instruction to my child or ask him another question?" By no means is this the case. Your child has to do many things every day of the week when you are learning the attending skill. At those times, you should continue to issue instructions to your child. Furthermore, there are many times you will want to ask your child a question. However, when you do this, be sure to listen to his response. Why ask a question if you are not willing to wait for an answer? Whenever you want to ask a question or give an instruction, consider whether your interactions with your strong-willed child involve too many instructions and questions, and whether one is necessary in this case. Many times attending is just as appropriate as issuing an instruction or question and far more effective in improving your relationship with your child.

If this seems difficult, don't despair. The five-week program for addressing strong-willed behavior does involve substantial effort on your part. As one of our grandfathers used to say, "There is no substitute for hard work!" Clearly, parenting is hard work, and changing the way you parent is even harder. Try to reward yourself every several days for accomplishing the assignments. Treat yourself to a video, a special lunch, or something else you enjoy. You deserve it!

It is important to learn this parenting skill in a play situation with your child. After learning the skill in this structured situation, you can begin using it throughout the day. By attending to your child throughout the day, you are letting him know you are interested in and acknowledging his appropriate behavior.

Please focus only on attending for the next seven days. Resist the temptation to read the next chapters! This program is most effective when you learn and practice only one skill at a time. Each subsequent skill builds on the previous skills. Parents who try to rush through the program and learn all the skills at once are often ineffective in changing the negative aspects of their child's strong-willed behavior. Your child's strong-willed behavior did not develop quickly, and it is not going to be changed quickly. Patience is very important!

7

Week 2: Rewarding

When you practice and use the attending skill, you are simply describing or imitating what your child does while he is playing or engaged in some other activity. The next skill you will learn—*rewarding*—is designed to make sure your child knows you approve of what he is doing. Rewards do not replace attending but rather build upon it. In other words, you should still describe your child's positive behavior but on some occasions move beyond this by also praising or rewarding the behavior. In this chapter, we will describe the kinds of rewards that are most important and explain how you can learn to use rewards effectively. In general, and as we indicated in Chapter 2, rewards may be social or nonsocial (material). Take a look at Table 7-1. Social rewards can be verbal, physical, or activity-based.

Verbal Rewards

Of all the rewards for young children, the most important are the *verbal rewards*, or praise. *Labeled verbal rewards*, in which you praise your child's behavior and label exactly what your child did that you liked, are of particular importance. For example, you might say, "Thank you for picking up your toys!" Think about that statement. Not only is your child being praised, but he also is being told the exact activity he

Types of Rewards	**TABLE 7-1**

Social Rewards

- Verbal: Praising your child's desirable behavior
- Physical: Providing physical contact (for example, a pat on the back) following your child's desirable behavior
- Activities: Doing activities selected by your child following his desirable behavior

Nonsocial Rewards

- Giving toys or treats following your child's desirable behavior

did (picking up the toys) for which he is being praised. So, you are both praising ("Thank you") and attending ("picking up your toys") to your child. Here are some other examples of verbal rewards:

- "I like it when you come to dinner when I call!"
- "I'm proud of you for playing so quietly!"
- "Thank you for picking up your blocks!"
- "I really like it when you obey me!"
- "Wow, you really did a great job of cleaning up your room!"
- "Thanks for helping me cook supper!"
- "I am really proud of you for doing such good schoolwork!"
- "You are a super kid for playing so nicely with your sister!"
- "Bob, I really appreciate that you came the first time I called you!"
- "I really noticed how hard you tried to stay by my side on our shopping trip!"
- "You popped right out of bed this morning when I called you! Thanks!"

In all of these examples, you are praising your child and labeling the desired behavior that occurred. For preschool children, this is extremely important. Parents need to be positive with children, but we also need to let them know exactly which behaviors we are praising. The more information and feedback we can provide to our children when we talk to them, the more they are going to learn appropriate behavior.

On some occasions you may not have the time or feel the need to label your child's exact behavior. In these cases, you can use brief comments, or *unlabeled verbal rewards*. Examples of these rewards include "Good job," "Great," and "Thanks." Again, each of these statements lets your child know that you approve of and are proud of his behavior. However, these general statements tend to be less effective.

For many of us, verbal rewards do not come naturally. Therefore, you might want to write on a note card some examples of verbal rewards you can use with your child. Keep the card with you and look at your list occasionally. This will help you remember ways to praise your child when he is behaving appropriately.

To use verbal rewards effectively, you have to consider not only *what* to say but also *how* to say it. Deliver praise in a pleased, enthusiastic tone of voice. Of course, some of us are not very expressive. If you happen to be this way, work on becoming more expressive when you are praising your child. A positive statement, such as "I really like it when you pick up your toys," is not very reinforcing if delivered in a monotone. Think about how you express yourself when you are really excited about something. That is how you should deliver verbal rewards to your child.

Our research indicates that, after reading this book, parents view verbal rewards as a relatively easy skill to learn and, importantly, as the most useful skill for increasing their child's appropriate behavior. This is really important information; however, it does not mean that learning to verbally reward your child's appropriate behavior will be easy—it will take thoughtfulness, dedication, and effort by you!

Physical Rewards

A pat on the back, an arm around your child's shoulder, or a wink at your child—these *physical rewards* let your child know that you like the behavior he is displaying. Hugs and kisses also can be used as physical rewards; however, it is better to use these expressions of love unconditionally with your child than to reserve them for rewards.

Think about how much positive physical contact you actually have with your strong-willed child. We have worked with many parents who do not like their child's behavior and therefore do not engage in much physical contact. If you are one of these parents, begin working on this by gently touching your child on the shoulder sometimes or patting him on the back. A simple wink or a playful tap can be very meaningful to a child. A realistic goal is to try to have twenty more touches per day with your child than you now have. You will be surprised how effective this can be.

Activity Rewards

When children have behavior problems, their parents tend to interact with them only when they have to. As you might guess, these times usually involve required tasks like bathing, meals, and bedtime. Unfortunately, this eliminates any chance for pleasant interactions around some activity your child enjoys. Using an *activity* he enjoys as a reward can be a very positive reinforcement for your child. It also gives you a chance to discover positive things about your child. Activity rewards might include playing a game, reading a story, or going on a walk. These activities can occur after your child has done something positive, such as picking up his toys or showing perseverance with a difficult task. But don't use these types of activities just as rewards—make time for fun activities with your child as much as possible. You will both enjoy yourselves and improve your relationship.

Activity rewards are a basic way of becoming more child-focused. This is important for you as a parent. The more you can focus on your child and become childlike in your own behaviors, the more you will enjoy your child, improve your relationship with him, and even find he is more eager to cooperate with you. Becoming childlike means doing things with your child that he enjoys doing—activities such as stacking blocks, going on a walk, throwing a football, playing with dolls, or playing video games. With all of these activities, you have to let go and get down to your child's level.

How do you decide what is a rewarding activity for your child? One way is to recall the things your child has asked you to do with him. Another is to simply ask him what he enjoys doing. You also might generate a list of activity rewards and let him know that these are things the two of you can do together whenever he completes certain tasks.

Nonsocial Rewards

Another type of rewards are *material*, or *nonsocial*, rewards— desirable objects such as toys or special treats. These types of rewards are sometimes useful when you start teaching a new behavior. However, nonsocial rewards should always be combined with praise. What is most important to your young child is your attention. In other words, simply giving a child a toy for good behavior will not be very effective in changing his behavior. Rather, your attention in the form of social rewards is most important and should be naturally linked to using nonsocial rewards.

The Smith and Jones Families

Let's rejoin the Smith and Jones families. In learning the skill of rewarding, they faced several challenges. However, they also enjoyed some successes.

The Smith Family

When we last visited Barbara and John Smith, they were beginning to experience more positive times with Tim and had realized the importance of describing Tim's good behavior. In contrast to the notion of attending, which was new to the Smiths, the notion of rewards certainly was not novel.

Both John and Barbara had read about the importance of rewards for positive behavior in various magazine articles about children. However, they had primarily thought of rewards as candy and toys, which they viewed as bribes for good behavior. The idea that attention served as a reward for children and adults was less familiar to them, and the idea that rewards were not bribery also was new. In particular, Barbara and John had never understood that the way to teach children to behave appropriately is to initially use rewards frequently for small changes in behavior, gradually require more behavior change in order to receive a reward, and once the behavior is learned, decrease the rewards as the behavior becomes maintained by internal gratification rather than external rewards.

Barbara and John found it easy to incorporate rewards into their daily practice sessions with Tim. However, incorporating rewards into their everyday routine was more difficult. In particular, both of the Smiths continued to think about disciplining negative behavior rather than focusing on Tim's less frequent positive behaviors. The two of them had to work together to develop a systematic plan before they could gradually change their focus from the negative to the positive aspects of Tim's behavior.

John and Barbara began by selecting one behavior, Tim's playing quietly while they had a conversation. They began to focus on when he did not interrupt rather than when he did interrupt. John, in particular, found this to be extremely difficult. His approach to handling any type of problem always had been to address it directly when it occurred rather than focusing on how to prevent the problem from occurring. Therefore, Barbara initially took the lead in working on Tim's interrupting behavior. Whenever John and Barbara engaged in a conversation, Barbara would turn to Tim and praise him for playing quietly. Initially, Tim looked at her in a puzzled manner and, on occasion, asked why she was talking like that to him. Before long he would simply look at her, smile, and continue playing. As Barbara continued to praise Tim for not interrupting, John gradually began entering in with positive comments of his own to Tim. Tim's interruptions of his parents' conversations occurred less and less often, and with time, the Smiths found they could praise less often than they did initially.

Once Barbara and John felt that they were focusing on the periods of time when Tim was not interrupting, they decided to begin rewarding a second positive behavior. By focusing on one behavior at a time and then moving to another behavior, the Smiths did not feel so overwhelmed by Tim's problem behaviors. Rather, they slowly but effectively addressed each of his behaviors that were causing difficulties in the home. Not surprisingly, Barbara and John found that with each new behavior they addressed, it became easier for them to use rewards for good behavior, and Tim's behavior began to change more rapidly.

Not only did Barbara and John begin rewarding Tim's good behavior, but they also began using the same skills with his sister, Susan. Her behavior improved even faster than did Tim's. Getting her to perform daily chores, like cleaning her room, required minimum effort by Barbara and John once they explained clearly to Susan what they meant by a clean room and praised her during and after she cleaned it.

John and Barbara Smith felt they were on a roll. They had a plan and could see positive change in Tim's behavior occurring in small steps. Furthermore, they were on the way to a more pleasant family life, including a better relationship between the two of them. Working together to effectively solve problems had more payoffs than they had anticipated!

The Jones Family

When we last tuned in to Patricia and Lisa Jones, more positive times were occurring between the two of them as Patricia used the attending skill. The concept of rewards came easily to Patricia, as she was receiving substantial attention in her career. Furthermore, the attention she received in her new dating relationship was a positive contrast to the lack of attention from Ed during their marriage. Thus, the idea of focusing on positive behavior, rewarding small changes in behavior, and using praise with Lisa made sense to her.

As with attending, what was difficult for Patricia was the time and energy to identify, focus on, and praise positive behaviors. With the help of some problem solving with her friend and confidante at work, Patricia decided to set aside several hours twice a week to engage in an enjoyable activity without Lisa or anyone else. Patricia felt that this time would allow her to clear her head and energize herself to focus more on Lisa's good behaviors. Patricia decided to resume horseback riding, an activity she had enjoyed before her marriage to Ed.

Patricia found horseback riding to be exactly what she needed. It was a time away from work and away from the daily hassles with Lisa. It allowed her to think about which of Lisa's behaviors she wanted to try to increase and how to use rewards to achieve this goal. Furthermore, it gave her a renewed energy for this task. The new rule Patricia applied during horseback riding was not to think about work but rather to let her mind wander for a while and then to focus on Lisa.

Patricia experienced some guilt over taking time for herself when she was so busy and already had so little time with Lisa. However, her friend pointed out to her that she was simply applying the parenting program to herself—she was rewarding herself for a job well done with Lisa and allowing herself time to plan how to be a more effective parent for Lisa. Viewing her own behavior in this way, Patricia was able to control her guilty feelings. Besides, for the first time in a long time, she was happy with herself as a mother at home.

Common Concerns About Rewards

Like the Smiths, many parents have concerns about rewarding. Perhaps the most common question is "Isn't using rewards with my child just a way to bribe him?" In fact, bribery and rewards are not the same. We all work for rewards—just think about the rewards, including financial compensation, you receive for doing a good job at work. In contrast, bribery is used to induce someone to do something bad or wrong, which obviously is not your goal in using rewards with your child.

Some authorities maintain that praise and verbal rewards are very different from encouragement. They view praise as being inappropriate, as it is used only when a child accomplishes something, and encouragement as being appropriate, as it is being used for effort or improvement. These authorities further believe that praise is based on competition and comparison, while encouragement is based on a child's assets and strengths. We disagree with this narrow view of praise. In our opinion, praise is used for effort and improvement and is based on a child's assets and strengths! We believe that many of the examples these authorities give of encouraging statements, such as "You really worked hard on that," are no different from praise. In short, we believe that the distinction between encouragement and praise is often arbitrary and semantic. Praise and encouragement are both social rewards used to increase desirable behavior. All social rewards, including praise and encouragement, are important. We encourage you to praise *and* encourage your child!

Another common concern about rewards is whether a child will depend on the rewards and have no self-motivation. In fact, rewards don't destroy self-motivation; they actually enhance it. The way we—as parents, teachers, or supervisors—teach any new behavior is initially through rewards. Once the behavior is learned, we gradually decrease the external rewards, and self-rewards (self-motivation) take over to maintain the behavior. Thus, your rewards teach your strong-willed child what behaviors you, as a parent, want to see occur more frequently. With time and an improved relationship between the two of you, he will perform these behaviors to please you and himself.

Finally, the experiences of many parents lead them to doubt the usefulness of rewards. Parents say, "I try to be as positive with my child as I can. I already have tried all those rewards, and my child's behavior is still terrible." True, most parents have made such attempts. But when rewards don't work, it is often because the parents have not learned and applied the principles of how to reward effectively—as outlined in this chapter.

How to Use Rewards Effectively

There are several important principles to follow when using rewards to change your child's behavior.

- As we have discussed, specify the behavior you are praising by using labeled verbal rewards.
- Use rewards immediately after the behavior you want to increase occurs.
- Initially reward small improvements in behavior and reward improvement every time it occurs.
- Reward only behaviors you want to increase in frequency.

By using labeled verbal rewards, you are providing your child not only with praise but with information about exactly what he did that led to the praise. This is how young children learn best!

You really cannot wait until later in the evening to let your child know that you appreciated his coming into the house in the afternoon when you called him. Effective rewards occur immediately after the desired behavior. Consequently, you need to be available and ready to praise your child *immediately* when he displays behavior you want to increase in frequency.

Initially it is also important to praise a child for small improvements in this behavior every time they occur. This sounds like a big job, and it is. However, consistent rewards for completing the first steps of a task prime the pump, so to speak, and get good behavior started. As time passes, your child's self-motivation will increase, and you can reward the completion of the final task rather than every step along the way.

Finally, praise only your child's good behavior in order to make clear that this is the behavior you want to see increase. This is very important. If you also acknowledge bad behavior, your child will not learn what you are trying to teach. Your strong-willed child may be one who has learned that in order to get attention, he has to behave badly. This principle of rewarding reverses the situation so that he gets attention when he is good and is ignored when he is bad. In the next chapter, we will present how to effectively ignore. For now, focus on rewarding behaviors you want to increase in frequency. Remember, in the five-week program, you learn one skill at a time!

The four principles for using rewards are important. Spend some time thinking about them and how you should use them when rewarding your child. Write them down on a note card and keep it in your pocket if this will help you remember the principles.

Learning to Use Rewards

Let's talk about how to begin using rewarding skills. Review the guidelines for the rewarding practice sessions summarized in Table 7-2. First, in the two ten-minute practice sessions you have each day, continue attending and begin rewarding. Verbal rewards do not replace attends but add to them—you should be using both skills in your practice sessions. If you used a tape recorder to record your attending sessions, continue to do this and listen to how you interact with your child. In particular, keep track of how many attends and verbal rewards you give. If your spouse or someone else can observe the sessions, as might have been done with attending, this also would be helpful. Either way, you need to receive feedback to make sure you are practicing this skill correctly. Many of us think we use these skills correctly and frequently; how-

Guidelines for Practice Sessions: Attending and Rewarding	TABLE 7-2

Do Not	**Do**
Issue any instructions	Attend to (describe) your child's appropriate behavior
Ask any questions	
Try to teach	Imitate your child's play behavior
	Verbally reward your child's appropriate behavior by praising him and labeling the desired behavior (For example, say, "Thank you for picking up your toys!")
	Tape-record the session or have someone observe the session
	Reward yourself for your efforts and performance

ever, when we receive some objective feedback, we are often surprised at how we are interacting.

Your goal, during the ten-minute practice sessions, should be at least verbal rewards and two attends per minute. Also, continue to work on issuing no more than four questions plus instructions during the ten-minute practice session. Most important, remember, even if you do not achieve these goals, you should focus on what you did right. Apply your rewarding skills to yourself—reinforce yourself for small improvements!

For the first three days, include rewards in your daily practice sessions. On the third day, also take ten minutes of private time by yourself or with your spouse. During this time think about three of your child's behaviors you would like to increase in frequency. This is an important point. Many people who seek help in parenting a strong-willed child are focused on finding out ways to decrease behaviors they do not like. At this point, you should instead focus on behaviors you want to see increase. For example, instead of thinking about ways to stop your strong-willed child from interrupting you

Focus on the Positive

You can benefit most from the powerful impact of praise if you concentrate on identifying the behaviors you want to increase in frequency.

Focus on sharing, not on snatching:

- Negative behavior: "Stop grabbing toys from your sister."
- Positive behavior: "While I was on the phone, I saw you share the toys with your sister. That was great!"

Focus on obedience, not on defiance:

- Negative behavior: "Why are you being so disobedient?"
- Positive behavior: "You put your shoes on so quickly when I asked!"

Focus on appropriate behavior, not on wild behavior:

- Negative behavior: "I wish you would stop running through the aisles of the grocery store."
- Positive behavior: "I'm pleased that you stayed by my side almost the whole time we were in the grocery store."

Focus on cooperation, not on tantrums:

- Negative behavior: "Your crying every time I ask you to get out of your bath is driving me crazy."
- Positive behavior: "Thank you for getting out of the bathtub quietly when I told you to get out."

and your spouse when the two of you are talking, think about ways to encourage your child to play quietly while you talk. Thus, the focus shifts from not interrupting to playing quietly, from disciplining your child for interrupting to rewarding him for playing quietly. Use of rewarding and attending is a powerful way to increase the positive behavior of your strong-willed child. Together, they help you find alternatives to punishing undesirable behavior.

During your ten minutes of private time, eliminate all distractions, including television, radio, and noisy children. Identify three of your child's behaviors that you want to see increase. These behaviors should be relatively simple ones that occur almost daily. If you find yourself thinking about behaviors you want to decrease, turn them around and look at the positive side of those behaviors. Instead of focusing on your child's ignoring instructions, focus on when he does follow instructions; instead of focusing on inappropriate forms of persistence such as stubbornness, focus on appropriate forms of persistence such as continuing to work on a difficult puzzle. Identify appropriate behaviors to increase, even if they occur only occasionally, rather than inappropriate behaviors to decrease. This approach takes being child-focused (an idea we discussed earlier) a step further—the focus is on your child's appropriate behavior.

Once you have identified the three desirable behaviors, pick one of them. Ideally, you should pick the one you feel most capable of increasing. That way you will be rewarded when your child's behavior improves. Next think about how you can use attending and rewards to increase that behavior. Examples of some behaviors to increase and the ways parents choose to increase them are presented in Table 7-3. Reading these might stimulate your thoughts and help you to see various ways to increase your child's positive behavior. Notice that you need to think through each situation and set the stage for appropriate behavior to occur. You cannot just wait for the desirable behavior to occur and then praise it. You need to develop a plan, focus on your child's positive behaviors, and praise them as soon as they occur. As we have said, parenting is hard work, but it pays off!

When you have selected the behavior and decided what you are going to do, the next step is to *do it!* See Worksheet 7-1 (page 100), which outlines the assignments you need to complete during the second week of the five-week program. When you have completed the assignments in Worksheet 7-1, you will be ready to move to the next skill. Note that one assignment in the worksheet, task 6, is not undertaken and completed until Week 3.

Over the next few days, begin using attending and rewards to reinforce the behavior you selected. When you have seen an improvement, select a second behavior from the three you wanted to change and begin working on it. Several

Desirable Child Behaviors and Ways to Increase Them	**TABLE 7-3**

Behavior	Suggested Procedure for Increasing Frequency of Behavior
Coming when called	1. Tell your child you want to work on improving his behavior when you call him. 2. Tell him exactly what you expect. (Say, for example, "When I call you, I expect you to stop what you are doing and come.") 3. Praise your child as soon as he comes in response to your call. 4. Praise him every time.
Staying with you in the grocery store	1. Tell your child you want the two of you to work on him staying with you in the grocery store. 2. Put your child in a shopping cart so he will stay with you. On the first trip, praise and attend to him every thirty seconds. 3. On the next few trips, let him walk beside you as you hold his hand. Praise and attend to him every thirty seconds. 4. On the next few trips, lightly rest your hand on your child's shoulder. Praise and attend to him every thirty seconds. 5. On later trips, have your child walk beside you with no physical contact. Praise and attend to him every thirty seconds. 6. Gradually lengthen the time between your praise and attending statements, but never phase them out completely.
Playing cooperatively with a sibling	1. Explain to both children that you want them to play together sharing the toys without arguing or fighting. 2. Monitor closely the play between the two children. 3. Praise appropriate play behavior.

days later, after you have moved into the next week of the program and the next skill, begin working on the third behavior. Continue to work on all three behaviors that you picked. In

Daily Assignments for Week 2: Rewards	**WORKSHEET 7-1**						
	Days						
Tasks	1	2	3	4	5	6	7
1. Two ten-minute practice times	☐	☐	☐	☐	☐	☐	☐
2. Selection of three behaviors to increase			☐				
3. Increase the first of three behaviors			☐	☐	☐	☐	☐
4. Consider the use of rewards throughout the day					☐	☐	☐
5. Increase the second of three behaviors						☐	☐
6. Increase the third of three behaviors					(Week 3)		

fact, you will probably always want to think about your child's behavior and decide whether there are behaviors you want to see increase. When we say always, we mean literally until your child leaves home to take a job or goes to college! As a parent of a young child, this may surprise you; however, we can assure you that there always will be room for improvement in your child's behavior. As your child grows, the behaviors will change. What will serve as a reward for him may change, but your focus on increasing the frequency of positive behaviors should never change.

Another assignment, which you should begin on Day 5, is to start thinking about how you can increase the use of rewards throughout the day with your strong-willed child (and then start doing it!). Again, this involves focusing on your child's positive behaviors rather than on his negative behaviors. All children demonstrate some positive behavior, and that is what we want to praise. When we experience difficulties with a child, most of us reach a point when we can see only the negative aspects of his behavior. If you have reached this point, deliberately focusing on the positive aspects of your child's behavior in your daily interactions with him can be difficult. However, by doing so, you can begin to improve his behavior as well as your interaction and relationship with your child.

There are countless situations in which you can use rewards with your child. Here are just a few examples to stimulate your thoughts about routine situations in which you may use rewards to increase your child's appropriate behavior:

- Riding in the car
- Watching television
- Preparing dinner
- Eating dinner
- Bathing your child
- Grocery shopping together
- Dressing in the morning
- Working in the yard
- Washing dishes
- Putting your child to bed
- Waking your child in the morning
- Playing games together

8

Week 3: Ignoring

As you begin Week 3 of the five-week program, continue your practice sessions and work on increasing the occurrence of the three behaviors you selected in Week 2. In addition, you will be adding a new skill to your parenting repertoire—one that will make the attending and rewarding skills even more effective. This skill is *ignoring*. It is used to decrease the occurrence of inappropriate behaviors. By attending to and rewarding appropriate behaviors and ignoring certain inappropriate behaviors, you will make it clear to your strong-willed child which behaviors you want to see more and which you want to see less.

How to Use Ignoring

Ignoring is basically withholding attention from children. It has three primary components:

1. **No physical contact.** Do not touch your child.
2. **No verbal contact.** Do not talk to your child.
3. **No eye contact.** Do not look at your child.

Obviously, you have to respond if your child does something dangerous or destructive. You cannot ignore behaviors like hitting, running into the street, or not following your instructions. We will talk about how to deal with these more "urgent" behaviors in Chapter 10. However, child behaviors that can be ignored include whining, tantrums, inappropriate demands for attention, and inappropriate crying.

For ignoring to be effective, you need to remove *all attention* from your child's behavior. This means you should not look at him, touch him, or talk to him. You should act as if you cannot see or hear him. You might even need to leave the room! Many parents have to leave when their child is having a tantrum or acting inappropriately. They go into a separate room in order to calm themselves.

Once you start ignoring a certain behavior, you must keep ignoring it. If you don't, your strong-willed child will learn that he can get your attention if he throws a bigger tantrum or whines long enough. Unfortunately, what normally happens is that when you first start ignoring a bad behavior, it actually gets worse! This happens because children sometimes think that they are not acting bad enough to get your attention. However, if you continue ignoring the behavior, the frequency of its occurrence is likely to decrease. If it does, the decrease is often fairly permanent, unless you start paying attention to the behavior again. Remember, attention can be physical contact, eye contact, or making some kind of comment.

To summarize, here are the basic principles of effective ignoring:

- Select a behavior that can be ignored.
- Remove all of your attention from the behavior when it occurs.
- Once you start ignoring the behavior, keep ignoring it.
- Expect the behavior to occur more often before it occurs less often.
- Reward and attend to appropriate behavior as soon as it occurs.

Think about how clear the message will be to your strong-willed child if you attend to and praise him for playing appropriately with his toys and remove all of your attention when he screams and cries. He receives attention for playing appro-

What Behaviors Can You Ignore?

Children sometimes engage in behavior that is annoying or bad-mannered but that does not pose a danger to anyone or damage anything. The best way to decrease the occurrence of that kind of behavior is simply to ignore the child when it occurs. Here are some examples of behavior that usually meets the criteria for ignoring:

- Inappropriately demanding attention
- Demanding you do something you do not want to do
- Crying for attention
- Throwing tantrums
- Whining
- Screaming
- Pouting
- Showing off
- Arguing
- Acting irritable

priately and no attention for acting inappropriately. Under these conditions, it will not take long for him to learn what behaviors you want to see!

Our research indicates that from a parent's standpoint, ignoring is a very difficult skill to use. One reason is that inappropriate behavior may increase initially before subsiding. This is hard for parents to take! Furthermore, almost all of us as parents want to take some kind of immediate action whenever our strong-willed children are behaving inappropriately. We feel we must respond in order to change our children's behavior or to show that we are good parents. In contrast, ignoring the behavior involves basically doing nothing. This is difficult! So don't feel bad if you have to remove yourself from the situation in order to force yourself to do nothing. You might go into the bathroom, close the door, and sit down for five minutes in order to gain control of yourself and not respond to your child's inappropriate behavior. However, you should remove yourself only if you are sure of your child's safety in your absence.

Although ignoring is difficult to use, our research also indicates that two months after completing the five-week program, parents see this skill as being as useful as the other four skills; what this means is that ignoring takes time, patience, and consistent use to be effective. However, when combined with attends and rewards for appropriate behavior, the use of ignoring for inappropriate behavior teaches your child which behaviors are and are not acceptable.

Can you help your child learn what you are doing when you use the ignoring skill? Yes—a good way to do this is to explain to him that you are going to ignore a certain behavior. Later in this chapter we will give you an example of exactly how to explain this to your child.

The Smith and Jones Families

Let's rejoin the Smith and Jones families and see what challenges and successes they experienced in learning the ignoring skill.

The Smith Family

When we last tuned in to the Smiths, Barbara and John were helping each other focus on Tim's positive behaviors. The next skill, ignoring undesirable behaviors such as disrupting their conversations, made logical sense. If attention is what a child wants, provide him with attention during the times when he is behaving appropriately and ignore his behavior when he is behaving inappropriately. Furthermore, telling Tim what behavior they would be ignoring and what behavior they would be praising would make it clear to him which behaviors are acceptable and which are unacceptable. However, using ignoring was no easy task for either of the Smiths.

John, in particular, found it very difficult to ignore disruptive behaviors. His idea was to address these behaviors straight-on with some act of discipline; however, he recognized that the program thus far had been quite effective and his previous efforts at eliminating problem behavior had certainly not been effective. Thus, once again, he was willing to try out the new skill. To help John, the Smiths developed a plan. Whenever Tim's behavior, such as throwing a tantrum and demanding attention, became so difficult to ignore that John felt he had to respond, he would remove himself to the bathroom and remain there for five minutes. This ensured that he did not respond and Tim received no attention. Furthermore, during John's practice times with Tim, Barbara would help John ignore inappropriate behavior by reminding him what to do and encouraging him to breathe deeply and think about something pleasant.

Through the Smiths' use of rewards for appropriate behavior and ignoring for inappropriate behaviors such as interrupting, crying, demanding attention, and throwing temper tantrums, Tim's behavior began to change slowly over the following days and weeks. Also, he seemed more content with himself as well as better able to control his emotions. His sister, Susan, even commented, "I don't mind Tim coming into my room sometimes now." The Smiths were really making progress!

The Jones Family

When we last tuned in to the Jones family, Patricia had decided to use horseback riding as a time to clear her head and spend time energizing herself to focus on Lisa's behaviors. As with the Smith family, the notion of ignoring made sense to Patricia, but she found it particularly difficult to ignore Lisa's tantrums. She felt she had very little time to spend with Lisa and, as a result, wanted there to be as little negative behavior as possible during these times. Rather than using the ignoring tactic, Patricia was inclined to provide Lisa with attention or whatever else would terminate her tantrums.

Patricia decided to work on ignoring one behavior at a time. Lisa often demanded attention from her mother and then had a tantrum if she did not receive it when Patricia was involved in other activities. Patricia selected this behavior to ignore. During one of her horseback-riding sessions, Patricia tried to figure out ways to prevent attention-getting behavior and tantrums from occurring, thus reducing how often she would need to ignore such behaviors (because they would occur less often). Patricia decided that spending more time with Lisa and focusing on her appropriate behaviors would leave less opportunity for the problem behaviors to occur. Furthermore, spending time with Lisa was actually enjoyable now.

Of course, Patricia knew she could not spend all of her free time with Lisa. She also knew this would not be healthy for either Lisa or herself. Thus, Patricia realized that she would need to use ignoring on at least some occasions. However, when tantrums did occur, Patricia did not feel as bad about ignoring Lisa because of the positive nature of their relationship at other times.

For Patricia, the tantrums that occurred in public places, like the grocery store, were the most difficult to ignore, primarily because they were so embarrassing. Patricia knew ignoring was the correct thing to do, but she worried about what others would think of her as a parent. Patricia finally resolved to "do what is correct." After explaining to Lisa which behaviors she would be ignoring and praising in the grocery store, Patricia increased her attention for appropriate behaviors, ignored tantrums, and ignored other people by turning her back and pretending to be closely examining the products on the shelf. It was not easy, but Lisa's tantrums gradually diminished, proving to Patricia that she had chosen the best course of action.

Learning the Ignoring Skills

During this week, your first assignment, beginning on Day 1 and continuing throughout the week, is to incorporate ignoring skills into your practice sessions with your child. Combine ignoring with rewarding and attending. Praise appropriate behaviors and ignore certain inappropriate behaviors, such as tantrums, whining, and inappropriate demands for attention. Thus, in your practice sessions, if your strong-willed child demonstrates undesirable behaviors you can ignore, remove all attention by turning your back and saying nothing to him

Guidelines for Practice Sessions: Attending, Rewarding, and Ignoring	**TABLE 8-1**

Do Not	**Do**
Issue any instructions	Attend to (describe) your child's appropriate behavior
Ask any questions	
Try to teach	Imitate your child's play behavior
	Verbally reward your child's appropriate behavior by praising him and labeling the desired behavior (For example, say, "Thank you for picking up your toys!")
	Ignore inappropriate behavior
	Tape-record the session or have someone observe the session
	Evaluate your performance
	Reward yourself for your efforts and performance

until his undesirable behavior totally stops. It may seem like forever; however, your actions will be a clear signal to him that you will not be attending to such behavior. Once the undesirable behavior stops, immediately turn back to your child and begin attending to and rewarding his appropriate behavior. Guidelines for practice sessions during Week 3 are presented in Table 8-1.

The second assignment, beginning on Day 2, is to pick out a behavior you feel you can ignore outside the practice sessions. This should be a behavior that occurs almost daily, such as those we have mentioned earlier in this chapter. When you have selected a behavior, sit down with your strong-willed child and explain that the behavior is unacceptable, you will ignore it, *and* you will give attention for appropriate behavior. Do everything you can to make it clear to your child which behaviors you want to occur and which you do not want to occur. Here is how one mother explained to her child a behavior she would be ignoring:

Johnny, you know how we have been working on how you and I get along with each other. We have been spending lots of time together, and I try to say lots of positive things when you are behaving well. Well, we are going to work on some different things now. You know how when I say, "No, you can't have a cookie," you sometimes scream and cry? Well, two things are going to happen. First, when I say, "No, you can't have a cookie," I really mean that you cannot have a cookie. Do you understand? Second, if you scream and cry, I am going to just walk away from you and not say anything to you. This is my way of saying that I don't like you screaming and crying when I say you can't have a cookie. When you don't scream and cry, I will be sure to let you know how proud of you I am.

The parent can then ask Johnny what she will do when he cries and screams and what she will do when he does not cry and scream. If Johnny does not yet understand, the mother can repeat what she just said and even role-play with Johnny. She can tell him to pretend to cry and scream. She can then walk away saying, "Johnny is screaming and crying. I am going in the kitchen."

By making sure the child understands what the parent is doing when she ignores him, learning which behaviors are and are not acceptable can occur more quickly. There are two additional important points to remember. First, explain each behavior you are going to ignore only once—it is easy for a child to trap a parent into continually discussing and arguing about problem behaviors. Second, remember to attend to and verbally reward appropriate behavior; unless this occurs, ignoring will not work.

Begin ignoring the selected behavior on Day 2. Work carefully to make sure you totally ignore this behavior.

On Day 5 select a second behavior to ignore. Follow the same procedure as before to explain what you will be ignoring, then begin ignoring the behavior.

Charting Your Success in Ignoring Inappropriate Behaviors	***WORKSHEET 8-1***					
	Days					
Behaviors to Ignore	*2*	*3*	*4*	*5*	*6*	*7*
1.	☐	☐	☐	☐	☐	☐
2.				☐	☐	☐

Using Worksheet 8-1, list the undesirable behaviors you hope to see less of by using the ignoring skill. Then indicate your success in ignoring undesirable behaviors. If you successfully ignored the behavior during any day, place a check in the box for that day. Remember, this process will take time, and it will not be easy! Also remember that for ignoring of tantrums and other similar behaviors to be effective, you also will need to praise appropriate behavior. Ignoring inappropriate behavior is effective only within the context of attending to and rewarding appropriate behavior.

Worksheet 8-2 outlines the assignments to be completed during the third week of the program. After you have followed these steps, you will be ready to move to the next skill.

Daily Assignments for Week 3: Ignoring	***WORKSHEET 8-2***						
	Days						
Tasks	*1*	*2*	*3*	*4*	*5*	*6*	*7*
1. Two ten-minute practice times	☐	☐	☐	☐	☐	☐	☐
2. Ignoring the first inappropriate behavior:							
Select first behavior		☐					
Explain to your child		☐					
Ignore the behavior		☐	☐	☐	☐	☐	☐
3. Ignoring the second inappropriate behavior:							
Select second behavior					☐		
Explain to your child					☐		
Ignore the behavior					☐	☐	☐

9

Week 4:
Giving Instructions

By this time in the program, you may have begun to notice changes in your strong-willed child's behavior. In particular, you may find that being with him is more pleasant and many of the interactions you have with him are less stressful than in the past. If so, then you are well on your way to a better relationship with your child!

The first three weeks of the program focused primarily on ways to improve your strong-willed child's behavior through changing your attention. By increasing positive attention toward your child, particularly when he is behaving appropriately, you increase the odds he will cooperate with you and comply when you give instructions. Those skills bring you to the phase where you can work directly on compliance. To do this, you must cultivate your skill in *giving instructions*.

Keeping Instructions Clear

In our clinical work with parents of strong-willed children, we have observed that parents often give instructions with which their child cannot easily comply. We have labeled these as *ineffective instructions*. Parents may give too many instructions at one time, give vague instructions, or actually distract their child from complying. They then become frustrated and angry with their child even though he really did not have a chance to comply. To avoid such problems with your child, you need to give clear and simple instructions, which we call *effective instructions.*

One way to recognize effective instructions is to compare them with types of instructions you do *not* want to use with your child. These are chain instructions, vague instructions, question instructions, "let's" instructions, and instructions followed by a reason. See Table 9-1. Each of these types of ineffective instructions makes it difficult for your strong-willed child to comply—just the opposite of what you want to happen.

Chain Instructions

If you say, "Get dressed, brush your teeth, comb your hair, and come downstairs for breakfast," you are actually telling your child to do four different things. This is an example of a *chain instruction*, which consists of giving several instructions at one time. The problem with a chain instruction is that your young child may not have the cognitive abilities to process this much information and remember all parts of the instruction. That is, your child may be unable to comply even if he wants to do so! You will have set up a situation in which noncompliance is likely to occur and you have not been fair to your child.

An effective alternative to giving a chain instruction is to break the instruction down into smaller steps and issue each part of it individually. For example, first tell your child to brush his teeth. When he has brushed his teeth, praise him and tell him to comb his hair. When he has combed his hair, use your rewarding skills to let him know you appreciate his following your instruction. By issuing instructions individually, rather than in a chain, you increase the chances of your child's complying.

Ineffective Instructions

TABLE 9-1

Type of Instruction	Definition	Likely Consequences
Chain Instruction	Instruction that involves numerous steps.	Your young child may not be able to remember all the things you told him to do. Therefore, he may not follow such an instruction.
Vague Instruction	Instruction that is not clear and may be interpreted by your child in a different way than you intended.	Your child may not be able to correctly interpret and follow instruction.
Question Instruction	Instruction in the form of a question, which gives your child the option of saying "no."	Asking your child places you in a position of having to accept "no" as an answer.
"Let's" Instruction	Instruction that includes the parent in completing the task when parent intends for the child to complete the task alone.	Child feels tricked and increases noncompliance.
Instruction Followed by a Reason	Instruction after which the parent gives the child a reason for the task.	A reason given after an instruction can distract a young child from complying. If you give a reason, keep it short and give it before you issue the instruction.

Vague Instructions

Children have difficulty with *vague instructions* because they are not clear or specific. Examples include "Be good," "Act nice," and "Behave like you should." The problem with this kind of instruction is that your child may not know what you actually want him to do. What you mean and what he thinks you mean might be very different!

It is much better to state directly what you want him to do. "Share your toys with your brother" is a better instruction than "Play nicely" or "Be good when you play together." The more specific you are, the more likely your child is to follow your instruction.

Question Instructions

Question instructions ask your child whether he will do something, rather than directing him to do so. For example, "Would you like to clean your room now?" is not a clear instruction. It creates a problem because your strong-willed child can—and probably will—simply say "no." If your intent is to give an instruction to your child and have him follow it, you should not phrase it in the form of a question and allow him the option of refusing. When a child says "no" to a question instruction, many parents become upset with their child for being defiant. However, the parents are really responsible for giving their child the option of refusing.

Instead of using question instructions carelessly, consider first if you really want to give your child the option of whether to comply. Asking, "Would you like to clean your room now?" is acceptable if you want to give your child the option of cleaning his room now or later. However, this is not what most parents mean when they use instructions in the form of a question. Unless you really mean for your child to have the option, avoid this type of instruction.

It is, however, important to give young children frequent options and choices so they can learn how to make decisions.

For example, from an early age, children should be given choices like what book they want you to read at bedtime, what clothes they want to wear, and within reason what they want to eat for a snack. However, it also is important to limit the choices of young children so that they are not overwhelmed by the options. The question "Do you want to wear your red or blue shirt today?" is easier for a young child to handle than "What do you want to wear today?" You want to give your child choices; however, be careful not to confuse questions and instructions.

"Let's" Instructions

A *"let's" instruction* is one stated in a way that includes the parent, for example, "Let's pick up your blocks now." If you actually intend to help your child pick up the blocks, this is an appropriate instruction. However, if your intent is for your child to pick up the blocks with no assistance from you, then a "let's" instruction is misleading and inappropriate. Your child may feel tricked and actually increase his noncompliance.

If your intention is for your child to do the task without your involvement, make this clear. You can say, "Pick up your blocks now." Stated this way, it is clear you will not be assisting in picking up the blocks.

Instructions Followed by a Reason

The last type of ineffective instruction is one that is *followed by a reason*. An example is "Pick up your toys because your grandmother is coming over, and you know how she likes a clean house." The problem with this type of instruction is that your child may forget the original instruction or be distracted by the reason that followed it. Remember, a young child's cognitive abilities are not developed well enough to retain the same amount of information that adults can. Giving a reason or rationale after you have issued the instruction may distract your strong-willed child, may cause him to forget what you originally asked him to do, or may lead to him questioning the reason you gave. As a result, he will fail to follow your instruction.

Giving a short reason or an explanation for a particular instruction is certainly appropriate, however. The effective way to do so is to give the reason first. Returning to the previous example, the parent might change the order of the instruction and the reason in the following way: "Grandmother is coming over, and she likes a clean house, so please pick up your toys now." In this way, the instruction is the last thing you say and the last thing your child hears. A child is more likely to comply with this instruction than one in which the reason follows the request.

Use Worksheet 9-1 to check whether you can already recognize different types of instructions. Read each instruction and decide whether it is effective or ineffective. Place a check in the box next to each effective instruction. If you believe the instruction is ineffective, write whether it is a chain, vague, question, or "let's," instruction or an instruction followed by a reason. Then compare your answers with the ones at the bottom of the worksheet. If you correctly identified at least nine of the statements, you have a good grasp of what makes instructions effective. Now you can begin to work on not using ineffective instructions.

We should note that other types of verbal statements than a reason after an instruction also can lead to your child not complying. The important point is to have the instruction be the last thing you say to your child. This will help him focus his attention on your instructions.

The Smith and Jones Families

Let's rejoin the Smith and Jones families and see what they discovered about the way they give instructions. As they learned to issue effective instructions, they faced a variety of challenges but enjoyed successes as well.

Identifying Effective and Ineffective Instructions	**WORKSHEET 9-1**

Place a check next to each statement that is an effective instruction. What makes each of the remaining instructions ineffective?

☐ 1. "Johnny, hand me the red block."

☐ 2. "Why don't you put on your coat now?"

☐ 3. "Please be careful."

☐ 4. "Please sit beside me."

☐ 5. "Put the red block here, and then put the green block over there."

☐ 6. "Johnny, you really need to be good when we play together."

☐ 7. "Because I want you to build a high tower, put the red block on top of the blue block."

☐ 8. "Put the red block on top of the blue block because I want you to build a high tower."

☐ 9. "Would you like to go to bed now?"

☐ 10. "Please clean up, put on your coat, and go outside."

☐ 11. "Let's pick up all the toys."

Answers: Numbers 1, 4, and 7 are effective instructions. Numbers 2, 3, 5, 6, 8, 9, 10, and 11 are ineffective. Numbers 2 and 9 are questions. Numbers 3 and 6 are vague. Numbers 5 and 10 are chain instructions. Number 8 is an instruction followed by a reason. Number 11 is a "let's" instruction.

The Smith Family

When we last tuned in to the Smith family, John and Barbara had changed much of their daily routine with Tim. They now were having regular playtimes, focusing on positive behavior throughout the day, and ignoring some inappropriate behaviors such as tantrums and demanding attention. However, some daily activities, such as picking up toys and taking a bath, still required the Smiths to issue instructions to Tim. Unfortunately, but not surprisingly, although Tim's relationship with each parent had improved and he did comply more than in the past, compliance with instructions was still a problem.

The idea of issuing simple instructions to Tim one at a time made sense to the Smiths. However, Barbara and John found that they had to remind each other not to give chain instructions and to give clear and specific instructions they were sure Tim could understand. John later said, "It was hard to think about giving straightforward instructions to Tim. I think I've always been afraid to tell him directly to do something because I knew he probably would not comply. Then I'd get angry and end up feeling bad."

Barbara and John began focusing on how they gave instructions to Tim. They thought about which instructions were most important for Tim to follow, and they only issued these in a simple and straightforward way. They also prepared Tim by warning him that new instructions were coming (for example, "In five minutes, you'll begin cleaning up.") and praised him as soon as he began showing signs of compliance. As they had with other skills, John and Barbara first focused on how they issued instructions in only one problem situation—toy cleanup in the afternoon. Next, they addressed how they issued instructions for taking a bath. It was beginning to be almost easy—solving one problem at a time by using both effective instructions and praise for compliance.

The Jones Family

When we last visited the Jones family, Patricia was rewarding positive behavior and ignoring Lisa's inappropriate behavior. Although the positive times with Lisa had definitely increased, Patricia still had some problems when she needed Lisa to do something immediately.

Patricia found the idea of simple and straightforward instructions very beneficial. She had to focus on Lisa when she was giving instructions and had to think carefully about how she worded those instructions. When she did this, Lisa appeared more responsive. Patricia found that she could avoid confrontations by letting Lisa know what to expect (by saying, for example, "In about five minutes, we will leave for school, and you will need to put on your coat."). Furthermore, she discovered that many of the instructions she was giving Lisa were really not important. Patricia found that she had given many instructions hoping that Lisa would comply occasionally. Patricia began to think carefully before giving instructions and decide whether each was important for Lisa to do. For those that were important, she then thought carefully about how to issue the instruction in a simple way. Because she often was pressed for time, Patricia also had to work hard to allow Lisa time to begin complying. However, one thing that did come easy was rewarding Lisa for compliance. This had become natural for Patricia!

In response to Patricia's simple and straightforward instructions coupled with rewards for compliance, Lisa's compliance in various problem situations improved substantially. However, by no stretch of the imagination was Lisa compliant all of the time.

Principles of Giving Instructions

By avoiding the five types of ineffective instructions, you—like the Smiths and Patricia Jones—will enhance the likelihood that your strong-willed child will comply with the request you make. Effective instructions will eliminate confusion for your child and increase the probability of compliance. So, exactly how should you give effective instructions? These are the critical components of that process:

- Think before giving an instruction, and make sure you are willing to work on gaining compliance regardless of the amount of time, energy, or effort required.
- Move close to your child, get your child's attention, make eye contact, and use his name before giving an instruction.
- Use a firm, but not loud or gruff, voice.
- Give an instruction that is specific and simple.

- Use physical gestures when appropriate (such as pointing to where to put the toys).
- Use "do" instructions rather than "don't" instructions.
- Wait quietly for five seconds after giving the instruction.
- Reward compliance.

Give only instructions you are prepared to follow through on to gain compliance from your child. If your child does not follow your instruction and you do nothing, what is going to happen? He will learn that you do not mean what you say, and his strong-willed behavior will increase. Thus, you need to be willing to follow through and use a consequence for non-compliance to your instructions. However, this is what you will learn in Week 5 of the program. For this week, just focus on how to give effective instructions.

First, before giving an instruction, make sure you have your child's attention. Ways to ensure that you have his attention are to move close to him, make eye contact with him, and use his name *before* you actually issue the instruction. To do this, you might say, "Johnny, I have something to say. Please look at me."

When giving an instruction, use a firm voice. It should not be loud or gruff, but it needs to be firm. Practice using a firm voice with your spouse, in front of a mirror, or on a tape recorder. You may be surprised at how you sound. Many parents sound as if they are begging their child to comply, while others, through gritted teeth, sound like a sergeant in the military. Neither style represents the firm voice we are proposing you use.

Use an instruction that is specific and simple. If possible, supplement your words with gestures such as pointing. For example, point to the bathroom if you are telling your child to wash his face.

Whenever possible, use positive instructions ("do this") instead of negative ones ("don't do this"). For example, when you and your strong-willed child are shopping together, you can say, "Stay by my side," instead of, "Don't run ahead of me." Using positive instructions creates a better relationship with your child and a better learning situation. It also makes it easy to praise your child for following your instruction.

Wait quietly for five seconds for your child to begin complying. Count silently from one to five to allow your child the opportunity to start complying.

Once your child begins to comply, use those attending and rewarding skills you learned during Weeks 1 and 2. By focusing on when your child initiates compliance, you can praise his compliance immediately. And, as we have stated repeatedly, praise will let your strong-willed child know which of his behaviors you want to see increase.

How do these principles fit with the first week of the five-week program (Chapter 6), in which you learned to use the attending skill? When you started working on attending, you also reduced the number of instructions and questions you used with your child. As you did so, you may have realized that you primarily spoke to your child using instructions and questions. But some situations do require giving instructions; so we now are focusing on making sure that each instruction you give is an effective one. In sum, children need fewer instructions and questions than we usually issue to them, but when you do tell your child to do something, you should make it an instruction with which he can comply *and* you should be willing to exert the effort needed to obtain compliance.

Learning to Give Instructions Effectively

Our research indicates that parents find giving effective instructions not only useful but also relatively easy to learn. However, like all the parenting skills in the five-week program, it takes practice.

During the first three weeks of the five-week program, you set aside two ten-minute periods per day to practice attending, rewarding, and ignoring. Now you have the option of replacing one of these periods with a ten-minute session in which you practice giving good instructions. However, you may choose to keep both ten-minute sessions for attending, rewarding, and ignoring and add a third ten-minute session to practice giving instructions. What's important is that you must keep *at least* one ten-minute session for attending, rewarding, and ignoring.

In the "giving instructions" session, tell your child that for this particular playtime, you will be expecting him to do as you say. You might say, "Sometimes we play the way you want to play. But right now I am going to be in charge and decide what we will do. I will be practicing telling you what to do." One thing he will learn from this is that sometimes it is his time to decide the rules and other times it is your time to decide the rules. Once you have established this, practice giving clear and simple instructions to your child. If you want ideas for instructions to give, you may want to look back to the Compliance Test in Chapter 5.

As you did during Weeks 1 through 3, tape-record your session or have someone record your instructions. In either case, use Worksheet 9-2 to count effective and ineffective instructions. Your goal is to give at least twenty instructions in a ten-minute period with three of every four instructions being effective ones.

During this daily instruction-giving session, praise your child for complying with your instructions. If he does not comply, simply ignore him for five seconds and then issue another instruction. As we indicated earlier, next week you will work on the consequences for not complying. For now, simply ignore noncompliance during the practice session because the purpose of these sessions is for you to practice giving effective instructions and praising compliance.

On Days 3 and 4, continue the same practice sessions and also pick out a daily activity that usually involves you giving instructions to your child. This may be dressing for preschool or school in the morning, or it may be your evening routine of bath time and preparing for bed. In whatever situation you choose, practice using simple, firm, clear instructions. Give

---

Record of Instruction-Giving

WORKSHEET 9-2

Tally the number of each type of instruction you issue each day during your practice session.

	Days						
	1	2	3	4	5	6	7
Effective instructions	—	—	—	—	—	—	—
Ineffective instructions: Chain instruction	—	—	—	—	—	—	—
Vague instruction	—	—	—	—	—	—	—
Question instruction	—	—	—	—	—	—	—
"Let's" instruction	—	—	—	—	—	—	—
Instruction followed by a reason	—	—	—	—	—	—	—
Total number of ineffective instructions	—	—	—	—	—	—	—

---

your child time to comply, and reward him for complying. If he does not follow your instructions, use whatever procedures you typically use.

On Day 5, select another situation that involves giving instructions to your child, and begin focusing on how you give instructions in that situation. Doing this will help you integrate what you have practiced into the instruction-giving sessions and into your daily routine. As we have emphasized repeatedly, integrating what you do in practice sessions into your daily interactions with your child will be necessary for your behavior to change and for his behavior to change. Giving good instructions is an excellent way to promote behavior change!

Worksheet 9-3 summarizes your assignments for Week 4. When you have followed these steps, you will be ready to move to the final week of the program.

Daily Assignments for Week 4: Instructions			WORKSHEET 9-3				
				Days			
Tasks	1	2	3	4	5	6	7
1. At least one ten-minute practice time for attending, rewarding, and ignoring	☐	☐	☐	☐	☐	☐	☐
2. One ten-minute practice time for issuing instructions	☐	☐	☐	☐	☐	☐	☐
3. Select the first daily situation in which to issue effective instructions and begin issuing instructions			☐	☐	☐	☐	☐
4. Select the second daily situation in which to issue effective instructions and begin issuing instructions					☐	☐	☐

10

Week 5: Using Time-Outs

By now you have built a better relationship with your child. Furthermore, he is complying more often with your instructions, in part because of your improved relationship and in part because you are giving effective instructions and praising his compliance. However, your child still will fail to comply at times. In this final week of the program, you will learn how to respond to your child's noncompliance. Let's first look at the importance of consistency in responding to this behavior.

Parents' Consistent Response to Noncompliance

As we indicated in Chapter 9, you must be willing to provide a consequence for noncompliance. In other words, your child needs to understand that he will experience a negative consequence for failure to comply, just as he experiences a positive consequence (praise) for compliance. You must be willing to use the consequence *every time* your child fails to follow your direction. If you do, he will quickly learn that you are not going to ignore or give in to his noncompliance. Once your child realizes that you are going to consistently use a consequence for noncompliance, he will have no reason to constantly test the limits by not complying.

Many parents are inconsistent in responding to their child's noncompliance. For example, one day you may have responded to his refusal to take a bath by saying, "OK, just be dirty if you want to," whereas on another day you may have said, "You are going to take a bath now, and I mean it!" This inconsistency in your reaction promotes further non-compliance because your child never knows what you are going to do, and he may test the limits to see exactly what you will do on any given occasion. In contrast, consistently using a specific consequence eliminates much of your child's limit testing and the related failure to obey.

Remember the context in which your child's noncompli-ance is now occurring. You have reduced the number of instructions you are giving; when you do issue them, they are clear and concise; and you are rewarding compliance. In this context, your child will likely comply much of the time, and, as a result, you probably will not have to apply consequences for noncompliance in many situations. This is evidence of the better relationship you now have with your child!

In our experience, most parents of strong-willed children have tried a variety of consequences for noncompliance and other problem behaviors. These consequences have ranged from ignoring to reasoning to threatening to spanking. Par-ents are often inconsistent in their use of these procedures as they switch from using one to another. Furthermore, each of these consequences poses a problem. While you can ignore attention-seeking behaviors such as whining or tantrums, you simply cannot ignore noncompliance or some other behaviors such as aggression or dangerous behaviors. If you ignore noncompliance or aggression, they will occur more frequently because they achieve their purpose and therefore are rein-forced. For example, if you ignore noncompliance, your child learns that he can avoid doing what you tell him to do. As a result, his noncompliance will pay off for him and will occur more frequently. In a similar fashion, physical aggression should not be ignored, not only because it is dangerous, but also because when ignored it will occur more frequently if it achieves its goal, such as hurting the person who is hit.

Reasoning is what most of us as parents would prefer to do. After all, if you could explain to your child why he should comply, wouldn't he do so? Unfortunately, reasoning rarely convinces strong-willed children. In fact, it does just the opposite: it rewards your child for noncompliance with your undivided attention! Threatening wild consequences ("You will never watch TV again as long as you live if you don't do what I say now!") will not work because your child knows you cannot carry them out (even if you want to sometimes). Spankings do more to vent parents' frustration and anger than to improve a child's behavior. In fact, the research data continue to accumulate showing that spanking can have long-term negative effects on children. In addition, spanking does not allow either parent or child to calm down, and it may teach a child that physical aggression is a way to solve a problem. This is not what you want your strong-willed child to learn! So, what is an alternative way to deal with your child's noncompliant behavior?

The consequence that we recommend you consistently use for noncompliance is *giving a time-out*. Research indicates that this procedure is a critical component of parenting programs for strong-willed children. *Time-out* refers to putting your child in a boring place for several minutes and withholding attention from him. In contrast to most forms of punishment, which involve doing something painful to your child, time-out is the removal of the opportunity to receive any attention. That is, rather than being a typical form of punishment, it is the *removal* of positive consequences. This can be just as effective as most forms of punishment without the negative side effects that many punishments have. And, as a result of the first part of the five-week program, your attention is now very important to your child, which will make removing attention through giving time-outs effective.

Effective Time-Out

Most parents have heard of time-out. Like many of the parents with whom we have worked, you may have even tried giving time-outs and concluded that it is not effective. But once we have shown parents the correct way to use time-out, their child's behavior does change, and they realize that giving time-outs does work. We think you will reach the same conclusion if you follow what we recommend in this chapter. Research has demonstrated that these procedures are the most effective ways of implementing time-out. It is important to follow them exactly as we present them. Minor changes can decrease the effectiveness of time-out significantly! Also, as you learn time-out, keep in mind that our research indicates that immediately after the five-week program, parents find time-out to be relatively difficult to learn and only moderately useful. However, over the following two months, parents report time-out becomes significantly easier to implement and more useful in dealing with their child's strong-willed behavior. This means you need to learn the time-out procedure and continue to use it—it will be effective, but it takes time and consistent use.

First, choose a location for giving time-outs in your home. There are a number of things you need to consider in choosing this place. It should be away from toys, people, windows, televisions, radios, and anything else your child enjoys. Remember, giving a time-out means your child is receiving no positive attention from you or anyone or anything else. Second, nothing breakable should be nearby. Why cause a disaster by putting your child in time-out next to a valuable lamp? Table 10-1 summarizes locations that are suitable and unsuitable for time-out.

One good place for time-out is at the end of a hallway. This is typically a place away from people and other enjoyable activities (for example, watching television). If you use a hallway for a time-out area, we recommend keeping an adult-sized chair in the time-out place. This can serve several useful purposes. First, it can remind your child that this is the

Choosing a *Time-Out Location*	*TABLE 10-1*

Best Options
- Hallway
- Kitchen corner (for two- and three-year-old children)
- Parents' bedroom

Least Desirable Option
- Child's bedroom

Not Options
- Bathroom
- Closet
- Dark room

time-out area. In addition, it helps you define where he should be during a time-out (that is, in the chair). Also, an adult-sized chair will keep your child's feet off the floor, so he will be less likely to get up during time-out. Be careful not to put the chair so close to the wall that your child can continually kick the wall, perhaps putting a hole through it.

A bedroom is also a possible location. Your child's bedroom may contain too many enjoyable activities, however. If it does and you absolutely must use your child's bedroom as the time-out area, remove all toys from the room. Your own bedroom may be a preferable location because it probably contains fewer things to entertain your child. Just make sure there are no breakables in the room.

For children who are two or three years old, a corner in the kitchen may be a good option. You can keep an eye on your child while he is in time-out. Be sure, however, not to make any contact (visual, verbal, or physical) with him.

Some parents identify a bathroom as a time-out area. This can be dangerous if it contains medicine, razor blades, or other potentially harmful objects. Consequently, we do not recommend using a bathroom as a time-out area.

Whatever location you select, never turn off the lights as part of giving a time-out. This will only scare your child. For the same reason, never use a closet or small, enclosed area for time-out. The purpose of giving a time-out is to remove your child temporarily from attention, not to frighten him.

The Time-Out Procedure

When you use time-out for your child's noncompliance, you need to follow an exact sequence for implementing the procedure. The steps to use are summarized in Table 10-2. Once you know the procedures and before you actually implement them with your child, you should explain to him exactly what will happen when he complies and does not comply. You should walk him through the entire sequence, from issuing a "pretend instruction" to which he "noncomplies," to going to time-out, to the "pretend instruction" being issued again. Remember, practice makes perfect! You can also go through each step of the time-out procedure and ask your child, "What will happen next?" The more your child understands the procedures, the more cooperative he will be when you use time-out, and the fewer times you will actually have to use it.

When you have given a simple and clear instruction, wait five seconds for your child to begin complying. If he does comply, praise him. If he does not, give one warning: "If you do not _____, you will have to take a time-out." Issue this warning in a matter-of-fact voice without yelling or becoming angry. Wait five seconds. If your child begins complying, praise him. If he does not, take him by the hand and say only, "Because you did not _____, you have to take a time-out." Say this only once and in a calm but firm voice. Do not lecture, scold, or argue with your child, and do not accept any excuses. Then lead your child by the hand to time-out. Do not talk to him while leading him to the time-out chair. Ignore shouting, protesting, and promises to comply.

When you tell your child he has to take a time-out, his response may trigger one of two problems. First, he may

Time-Out Sequence for Noncompliance	TABLE 10-2

1. Issue an effective instruction.
2. If your child does not begin to comply within five seconds, issue a warning: "If you do not _____, you will have to take a time-out."
3. If your child does not begin to comply within five seconds, state, "Because you did not _____, you have to take a time-out."
4. Lead your child to time-out without lecturing, scolding, or arguing.
5. Ignore shouting, protesting, and promising to comply.
6. Tell him to sit in the time-out chair.
7. When he is sitting quietly, set the timer for three minutes.
8. When his time is over, including being quiet for the last fifteen seconds, return to the chair and tell him time-out is over.
9. Restate the original instruction.
10. Implement the time-out procedure again if your child does not comply.

immediately begin complying. If he does, do not give in but move ahead with implementing time-out. This is difficult because, after all, he did finally comply. However, think about what he will be learning: "I don't have to comply until my mom gives me an instruction, a warning, and then starts to take me to time-out." Obviously, this is not your goal. Second, your child may resist going to time-out when you start to lead him to the chair. If this occurs, you have several options. First, you can stand behind him, put your hands in his armpits, lift him up so that he is facing away from you, take him to the time-out chair, and put him in the chair as you stand behind it. Second, for a child who is five or six years old, you can tell him that he will lose a privilege. (See the section "Overcoming Time-Out Problems" later in this chapter for more information.) Third, you can tell him you are going to add three more minutes to time-out (six minutes instead of three minutes). Then try again to lead him to time-out, and set the timer for six minutes. If you still cannot get him into the time-

Consequences for Compliance and Noncompliance

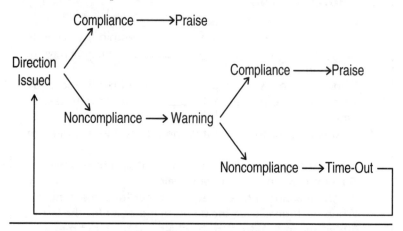

out chair, do not keep adding three minutes. Try either the first or second (if your child is five or six years old) option. When you and your child reach the time-out chair, tell him to sit down. When he is quiet, you can set a timer and tell him to stay in the chair until the timer sounds. A timer is not necessary, but it can provide your child with a cue about the length of time-out. Place the timer where he can see but not touch it. Set the timer for three minutes (unless you lengthened it to six minutes).

The length of the time-out should depend, in part, on a requirement that your child be quiet before you end the time-out. When you first begin using time-out, require your child to be quiet for the last fifteen seconds of time-out. If he is screaming or kicking the wall at the end of his time-out period, wait until he has been quiet for at least fifteen seconds beyond the time-out period before removing him. After several weeks of using time-out, you can change the requirement so that your child has to be quiet for the last minute of time-out. You can gradually continue to lengthen the time he has to be quiet before leaving time-out. In this way your child will learn that good behavior in time-out is important and is required for leaving time-out. Do not end the time-out until your child is quiet!

After the time-out period is over, return to the chair and tell your child that he may get up. Since he had to go to time-out for not following an instruction, return to the scene where he initially failed to comply, and give the original instruction again. You must do this, or he will learn that he can get out of following your instructions if he takes a time-out. If your child goes to time-out for refusing to pick up toys and you pick them up while he is in time-out, he will learn that he can avoid picking up his toys by taking a time-out. Once he is out of time-out and you have issued the instruction again, follow the same sequence leading to time-out if he does not comply.

The flowchart "Consequences for Compliance and Non-compliance" shows the different pathways and consequences for each pathway that you should apply depending on whether or not your child complies with your instructions. Remember, after giving a time-out, you always return to issuing the instruction again. Theoretically, you could stay in the sequence forever if your child never complied. However, we recommend that you continue this sequence only until your child complies or he reaches his eighteenth birthday (just kidding!). Seriously, you must stick with it until he complies, and he will when he becomes aware of your determination. As soon as he complies, praise him!

Some parents want to spend time discussing in detail with their child why time-out was used, their love for the child, and how horrible it made them feel to have to give a time-out. Other parents want to have a discussion with their child in order to induce guilt over not complying and receive an apology from the child. Neither of these two types of discussion is desirable or helpful. A brief comment, such as "You had to go to time-out because you did not do what Mommy told you to do," but no more, is acceptable after time-out.

Overcoming Time-Out Problems

You may encounter several problems when using time-out. One of the most common is that your child may not stay in the time-out chair when you tell him to do so. If this happens, you have several options. First, if he initially refuses to sit or stay in the chair, you can tell him that the time-out period will not even start until he sits down in the chair. A second option for refusing to stay in the chair is to add three minutes to the time-out (six minutes instead of three minutes). As with refusal to go to time-out, do not keep adding minutes to time-out each time the child leaves the chair. Instead, set the timer for six minutes each time your child is returned to the time-out chair. A third option is that you can place him in the chair again, tell him to "Stay in the chair," and place your hand on his leg to encourage him to remain seated. A fourth option for a child who is five years of age or older is to tell him that if he does not return to the time-out chair, he will lose a privilege. For example, you could say in a calm voice, "If you get up again, you can't ride your bike the rest of the day." Remember, if you say it, do it! Removing privileges will not work with children younger than five because they have difficulty bridging the gap in time between what is happening now and enjoying the privilege later.

Another common problem is that your child may say things in time-out that are meant to get your attention. Some of these may be painful for you to hear. Here are some of the most common statements that parents hear:

- "I have to go to the potty."
- "I don't love you anymore."
- "I'm going to run away."
- "I hate you."
- "I like time-out better than being with you."
- "You are ugly and mean."
- "I wish I was dead."
- "I am going to call 911."
- "I wish you were not my mommy."
- "I wish you were not my daddy."

You just have to ignore these statements!

Some parents report that while their child sits in the chair, he pushes the chair slowly out of the time-out area with his feet. This is one reason for using an adult-sized chair in time-out. With such a chair, your child's feet can't touch the floor. Therefore, in order to push the chair out of the time-out area, he has to be out of the chair. In that case, follow through with one of the four options we presented for handling a child who leaves time-out.

Sometimes a child refuses to come out of time-out when it is over. If this occurs, you need to take control and tell him that you are imposing another time-out. After all, refusing to leave time-out is another case of not complying. Set the timer for three minutes again. When the timer goes off, return to the time-out area and again tell him that he should leave time-out. If he still refuses to come out of time-out, start the timer again. Do this until your child agrees to come out and follow the instruction you originally issued. He will eventually agree!

Table 10-3 summarizes these and other time-out problems and solutions. Giving time-outs is a complicated procedure, so you will need to practice it before using it with your child and then go over it with your child, including walking him through the entire procedure. Toward the end of this chapter, we will spell out how to learn, practice, and use time-out for noncompliance.

Using Time-Out for Other Problems

The time-out procedure you are learning can be used not only to handle noncompliance but also with other behavior problems that you cannot ignore. You need to respond by using a time-out when your child does any of the things in the following list. (Continue to ignore behaviors that you identified in Week 3, such as crying, tantrums, and demands for attention.)

Time-Out Problems and Possible Solutions	**TABLE 10-3**

Problem	**Possible Solutions**
Refusing to sit in the chair	• Do not start the time-out until he is seated.
Leaving or moving the chair	• Stop the timer until your child sits down.
	• Add three minutes to time-out, and reset the timer for six minutes.
	• Place your child in the chair, tell him to stay, and place your hand on his leg.
	• Remove a privilege if your child does not return to the chair (for children aged five years old and up).
Insulting you verbally	• Ignore the insults.
Yelling and crying	• Ignore the yelling and crying.
Refusing to leave time-out	• Start time-out over.
A sibling interacting with your child while he is in time-out	• Put the sibling in time-out in another location.

- Hitting a sibling, playmate, or parent
- Running into the street
- Jumping on furniture
- Biting another child
- Destroying household objects or the toys of another child
- Using bad language
- Talking back to a parent or another adult
- Kicking, slapping, pinching, or pulling hair
- Throwing objects that are not meant to be thrown

The most effective response to these behaviors is a time-out procedure similar to the one presented for noncompliance.

Explaining House Rules: An Example

Here is how one mother explained house rules to her four-year-old child:

"Johnny, let's turn off the TV and talk for a few minutes. You know I have been getting upset with you sometimes around the house. I think one way to help you behave more and for us to get along better is to set up some house rules.

"House rules are rules that you always should obey. If you don't obey a house rule, you will have to immediately take a time-out. If you break a house rule, I will tell you what you did, take you by the hand, lead you to time-out, and have you sit in time-out for three minutes. Let's practice going to time-out after breaking a house rule. [They practice the procedure just described.]

"Now, see this piece of paper? On the top is written 'house rules.' I am going to write down three rules and put some pictures on it to show what you can and cannot do. The rules are

1. No jumping on furniture.
2. No hitting your sister.
3. No running in the house.

"Anytime you jump on the furniture, hit your sister, or run in the house, what will happen? That's right, you immediately will have to go to time-out. Tell me what the rules are." [She waits for child's response.]

"Now I am going to put the list here on the refrigerator. Every morning I will remind you of the rules.

"OK, now that we have set up some rules, let's go outside and toss your ball."

Depending on your child's age, adapt this approach to the rules and needs of your own household.

However, the procedure will differ in several ways. First, tell your child only one time not to engage in any of these behaviors. Tell him that if he does the behavior, time-out will immediately occur. Also, because these behaviors do not involve you giving him an initial instruction, state your expectations by developing a list of "house rules." If your child violates a house rule, never issue a warning. Instead, use time-out immediately.

Tell your child in advance which behaviors will result in immediate time-out. Prepare for this by listing no more than three house rules and posting them on the refrigerator or some other location where your child can see them. For a young child who cannot read, present the rules in the form of pictures. Read the rules to your child, and review the time-out procedure for breaking the rules. Show him the time-out chair. Walk him through what will happen when he displays any of the behaviors. Have him repeat the list of behaviors and the procedure to make sure that he comprehends them. By making sure he understands what behaviors are acceptable and unacceptable and what will happen when the house rules are broken, you are being fair to him. Also, remind him each day about the house rules.

At the end of a time-out for breaking one of the house rules, say, "You had to go to time-out because you broke a house rule. Which rule did you break?" If he responds correctly, say, "That's right. Don't _____ again." If he responds incorrectly or does not respond, briefly tell him what rule he broke. Next, immediately try to involve your child in an activity (such as helping you do a task) so you can praise him.

You can also use time-out for noncompliance and other problem behaviors outside of the home. However, use it in public places only after you have successfully used it at home. The main difference in using time-out outside the home is that you have to identify an appropriate location. If you are shopping, you can use a corner of the store or the backseat of your car. For example, if your child becomes disruptive, you can give him a warning: "If you do not keep your hands inside the shopping cart, you will take a time-out in the car." If your child does not comply, take him by the hand and lead him from the store. Place him in the backseat of your car and turn your back while standing outside the car. Make sure you have the keys to the car! Leave him in the car for the length of his time-out, then open the door and take him back into the store. Praise him as soon as he is behaving. When you use your car to give a time-out, never leave your child alone, and make sure the temperature in the car is appropriate for a child.

The Smith and Jones Families

Using time-outs helped the Smith and Jones families manage noncompliance and other problem behaviors. Read on to find out how.

The Smith Family

When we last visited the Smith family, Tim's relationship with each parent had continued to improve. Furthermore, as his parents issued instructions in a simple and straightforward manner, Tim's compliance was improving. However, he sometimes said he would comply (saying, for example, "I will pick up my toys in a minute") but did not do so. At other times, he refused to comply (saying something like, "No, I don't want to pick up my toys!") or even threw a tantrum rather than comply. Barbara and John therefore welcomed the chance to use time-outs.

In the past, Tim's parents had handled his problem behaviors such as noncompliance by imposing a variety of consequences. These consequences had included pleading, threatening, screaming, and, on some occasions, spanking. Neither Barbara nor John had found any of these consequences to be effective. Switching from one type of discipline to another in order to "make the punishment fit the crime" just had not worked. Furthermore, Barbara and John usually felt bad after screaming, threatening, or spanking. So the Smiths liked the idea of using time-out for every act of noncompliance and for other behaviors that could not be ignored.

Tim was a creative child. When his parents began using time-out, he pushed every limit. He moved the time-out chair around the room without actually leaving the chair, refused to get out of time-out when the time period was over, claimed he was going to wet his pants while sitting in time-out, and shouted, "I hate my mom!" when in time-out. However, the Smiths were equally creative problem solvers. Each time Tim tried a new trick to disrupt time-out, John and Barbara sat down and discussed how to handle it.

Gradually, time-out became a straightforward procedure that the Smiths used for occasional instances of noncompliance and as a way for Tim to calm down when he became upset and disruptive. In fact, Tim sometimes would even put himself in time-out in order to calm down when he became upset with his sister. He was beginning to find ways to control his own behavior to keep himself out of trouble.

The Jones Family

When we last visited the Jones family, Patricia had realized there were many instructions she did not need to give to Lisa. Patricia also noticed that when she did give instructions, Lisa would comply if they were simple, logical, and straightforward. For Patricia, time-out was not a new concept. However, she learned that she had not been using time-out appropriately. Patricia had always felt it was important to lecture Lisa before and after time-out in order to make sure Lisa understood what was wrong about her behavior. She later explained, "It seemed logical to me to spend time with Lisa going over and over what was wrong with her behavior. That's why I never thought time-out worked. Time-out with lots of lectures appeared to only increase her bad behavior. I never realized I was giving her attention when the whole purpose of time-out was to keep her from receiving attention."

Patricia sat down with Lisa and explained the time-out procedure, when it would be imposed, and exactly for what behaviors it would be imposed. She then walked Lisa through the time-out procedure and, with questioning about each step, assured herself that Lisa understood time-out. After that, she rarely had to use time-out. Lisa no longer needed to push her mother in order to see what she could get away with.

Practicing Your Time-Out Skills

Worksheet 10-1 summarizes your daily assignments for using time-out with your child's noncompliance during Week 5. It

Assignments for Week 5 and Beyond: Using Time-Outs	**WORKSHEET 10-1**						
	Days						
Tasks	*1*	*2*	*3*	*4*	*5*	*6*	*7*
1. Select time-out place	☐						
2. Memorize the steps of time-out	☐						
3. Practice giving time-outs with another adult and without your child	☐	☐	☐				
4. Tell your child about time-outs for noncompliance			☐				
5. Begin giving time-outs for failure to comply with one instruction				☐	☐	☐	☐
6. Begin giving time-outs for failure to comply with all instructions							☐
7. Begin giving time-outs for other problem behaviors in the home (Beginning Week 7)							
8. Begin giving time-outs for problem behaviors in public places (Beginning Week 9)							

also provides for practice in using time-out to manage other behaviors in the home and in public places. As you carry out these assignments, remember to continue at least one ten-minute daily practice session in attending, rewarding, and ignoring.

Start on Day 1 by selecting a time-out place and memorizing the time-out procedure. On the first three days of this week, learn the time-out procedure by studying and practicing as described below. Plan to allow at least thirty minutes a day. Remember, time-out is complicated! Reread this chapter, in particular Tables 10-2 and 10-3. Practice the time-out procedure with your spouse or some other adult by completing the following tasks:

1. Describe where and why you selected a particular location for time-out.
2. Describe the time-out procedure step-by-step as it is presented in Table 10-2 and described earlier in this chapter.
3. Describe how you will handle problems that arise in time-out as presented in Table 10-3.
4. Walk the adult through the entire time-out procedure as presented in Table 10-2. Note any mistakes you make, and go through the entire procedure again.
5. Walk the adult through the entire time-out procedure but have him or her display problem behaviors going to and in time-out. Note any mistakes you make handling these problems, and rehearse again.

On Day 3, go over the time-out procedures as described in Table 10-2 with your child. Walk him through the entire time-out procedure so he will know exactly what to expect and ask him questions about "What will happen next?" Tell him about two important rules he must follow when in time-out: (1) stay in the time-out chair without his feet touching the floor and (2) remain quiet.

Select an instruction that you often issue to your child and that he often fails to follow. Tell him that time-out will occur every time he does not follow this instruction. Then, using the time-out procedure from Table 10-2, give your child a time-out whenever he does not follow the instruction. After using time-out with this behavior on Days 3 through 6, tell your child that all failure to follow instructions at home will result in time-out. Begin using time-out with all such noncompliance.

Post two things on the wall where you will see them every day: a copy of the time-out procedure in Table 10-2 and a calendar. Refresh your memory daily by reading the time-out procedure. On the calendar, record each time you use time-out and the behavior for which you used it. This will help you keep track of how often you use time-out and whether your child's strong-willed problem behaviors are changing.

After two weeks of using time-out in response to non-compliance, begin using it with other problem behaviors you cannot ignore in the home. Set up and explain house rules for these behaviors. Post your house rules, in picture form for a child who cannot read, on the wall or refrigerator. After about two more weeks of using time-out for problem behaviors in the home, begin using it outside the home.

Learning the details of the time-out procedure will take your full attention. In fact, you will have to be a little strong-willed yourself in order to use it effectively. And, as our research indicates, it takes time for you to feel comfortable with the use of time-out and for it to be effective. However, if you are attentive to your child and reward compliance, you should not have to use time-out very often. Be careful not to revert to focusing only on your child's problem behaviors. Attending and verbally rewarding will build the positive relationship you want to have with your child.

11

Integrating Your Parenting Skills

Effectively parenting a strong-willed child requires continual effort. Therefore, to help you review the assessment process and the five parenting skills taught in Part II, we have summarized them in Table 11-1. You can use each of these skills as tools to improve your strong-willed child's behavior.

Combining Your New Skills

The skills in the five-week program for addressing strong-willed behavior should be integrated with one another. Together, these skills provide three basic ways to change strong-willed behavior:

1. You can increase the occurrence of cooperative behavior, which is often incompatible with strong-willed behavior problems, by attending and rewarding.
2. You can decrease the occurrence of strong-willed problem behavior by removing positive reinforcement for problem behavior through the use of ignoring and giving time-outs.
3. You can reduce noncompliance (a frequent aspect of strong-willed behavior) by modifying what you do before the behavior—that is, *how* you issue instructions to your child.

The Assessment Process and Five Parenting Skills	TABLE 11-1

Assessment Process

- Does my child's behavior need to change?
- Does he often display problem behaviors common among strong-willed children?
- Is his behavior a problem in daily situations?
- Does he score poorly on the Compliance Test?
- Am I often frustrated with his behavior?

Skill 1: Attending

- Describe your child's appropriate behavior.
- Imitate your child's play behavior.
- Reduce directions, questions, and attempts to teach.
- Practice!

Skill 2: Rewarding

- Continue to describe and imitate your child's appropriate behavior.
- Verbally reward your child's appropriate behavior by praising him and labeling the desired behavior.
- Practice!

Skill 3: Ignoring

- Decide which behaviors you can ignore.
- When your child misbehaves in a way that can be ignored:
     Make no physical contact.
     Make no verbal contact.
     Make no eye contact.
- Practice!

Skill 4: Giving Instructions

- Get your child's attention and make eye contact.
- Use a firm, but not loud or gruff, voice.
- Give an instruction that is specific and simple.
- Use physical gestures when appropriate.
- Reward compliance.
- Practice!

| **TABLE 11-1 continued** |

Skill 5: Using Time-Outs

- Choose a time-out location.
- Memorize the steps of time-out.
- Practice without your child.
- Tell your child about time-out for noncompliance and other problem behaviors.
- Begin giving time-outs in the home.
- Begin giving time-outs outside the home.

It is through the *combined* use of these three concepts that you will most effectively improve your child's strong-willed behavior. With any behavior problem, you need to assess what you are doing *before* the behavior and what you can do more effectively *after* the behavior. After the behavior, most of your solutions should combine skills (attending and rewards) to increase desirable behavior, with the use of ignoring or time-outs to decrease negative strong-willed behavior.

Let's look at an example. Suppose you are having difficulty with your child in the grocery store. He is demanding candy and running away from you when you do not let him have it. To assess how you are handling this situation, ask yourself questions that concern your use of each of the skills for changing negative strong-willed behavior: Am I attending to and rewarding my child's cooperative behavior? When he does demand candy, am I telling him "no" and then ignoring his behavior? Have I told him running away from me will result in a time-out, *and* am I actually giving him a time-out for such behavior? When we enter the store, am I giving him clear instructions concerning the behavior I expect from him? By answering these questions, you identify what you are doing and what you should be doing. In this way, you are considering all five of the skills taught in the program and how to combine them to address one of your child's particular strong-willed behaviors.

In our clinical work, we talk to parents about the importance of consistency in using the skills taught in the five-week program for addressing strong-willed behavior. If you *consistently* acknowledged your child's positive behaviors through attending and rewards, ignored minor inappropriate behaviors, issued clear instructions, and gave time-outs for inappropriate behaviors that cannot be ignored, you would be the perfect parent! Under these conditions and within the context of your child's temperament and your broader family environment, you would achieve the maximum possible change in your child's negative strong-willed behavior. However, we have never met or heard about the perfectly consistent parent, and you are not likely to be the first one. Instead, work to be as consistent as possible, but realize that you will not be perfect.

The Smith and Jones Families

After their parents participated in the parenting program, were Tim Smith and Lisa Jones "perfect" children? Of course not. Especially in Tim's case, the Smiths had to continually regroup and return to the basics of the program to solve new problems. This required them to discuss each new problem, develop a plan using the skills they learned in the program for handling the problem, and work together to implement the plan. This strategy did not eliminate each new problem behavior, but they were able to diminish the problems. Barbara and John knew Tim would never be as easy to manage as his sister, Susan; however, they began to feel competent as parents and ready for the birth of their third child.

Although Lisa was not perfect either, Patricia did not have to solve problems nearly as often as the Smiths did. When Patricia had finished the five-week program, Lisa's behavior continued to improve, with few setbacks. But like the Smiths, Patricia became a long-term problem solver and began to feel competent as a parent.

The Five Skills in Context

As the Smith and Jones families learned, using the parenting skills of the five-week program for addressing strong-willed behavior does not get perfect results. That is partly because no parent is perfect. Also, parents must exercise those skills within a larger context. As summarized in Table 11-2, a child's behavior is influenced not only by the responses of his parents but also by his temperament and the overall home environment.

You will be most effective as a parent if you use the skills from the five-week program within a context of creating a solid foundation for behavioral change. As we will present in Part III, this involves changing the nature of your family life, developing communication skills and patience, and building your child's self-esteem and social skills. For example, if you use the parenting skills but fail to develop patience or effective communication with others, your child's strong-willed behavior will be more resistant to change. Parenting skills such as those taught in the five-week program are necessary for changing your child's negative strong-willed behavior, but these skills alone are not sufficient. Creating a solid foundation for behavioral change is also necessary.

Your child's temperament (the topic of Part I) also cannot be ignored. You can consider his temperament an indicator of how much effort will be required to change his undesirable strong-willed behavior. The more difficult your child's temperament in such areas as persistence, reactivity, adaptability, and emotionality, the harder you will have to work to change his negative strong-willed behavior. Furthermore, his temperament also may determine how much change in his negative strong-willed behavior you will achieve. A very difficult temperament probably limits how much change will occur in his behavior. In essence, your child's temperament should be an important indicator of your expectations for his behavior. For that reason, Barbara and John Smith had different short- and long-term expectations for Tim (a child with

TABLE 11-2

The Context of Strong-Willed Behavior

Dimension	Broad Role	Ways Each Dimension Fulfills Its Role
Temperament	Sets stage for strong-willed behavior	• Defines amount of effort that will be required to change negative strong-willed behavior. • Helps define expectations for changes in your child's strong-willed behavior.
Parenting Skills	Address strong-willed behavior problems	• Attends to positive behaviors. • Rewards for positive behaviors. • Ignores minor inappropriate behaviors. • Gives appropriate instructions. • Uses time-outs for inappropriate behavior.
Positive Family	Facilitates the change of strong-willed behavior	• Teaches adaptive handling of family stressors. • Sets routines, traditions, and rituals. • Uses good communication skills inside and outside of the home. • Focuses on having fun with your child. • Decreases screen time. • Increases your child's creative play. • Stresses the importance of family meals. • Develops more patience. • Builds your child's self-esteem and social skills.

a difficult temperament) than Patricia Jones had for Lisa (whose temperament was less difficult).

To review the dimensions of strong-willed behavior, temperament can be viewed as laying the groundwork. That is, it can set the stage for strong-willed behavior to develop, it informs you of how hard you will have to work to change behavior, and it indicates what expectations for changing your child's strong-willed behavior are reasonable. Within this context, you can apply the skills you learned from the five-week program for addressing strong-willed behavior. When used in combination, these skills can lead to changes in your child's strong-willed behavior within the limits defined by his temperament. Finally, a negative family environment will hinder improvement in your child's strong-willed behavior. In contrast, a positive family environment will make such change easier. Making your family life more positive is the focus of Chapter 12 in Part III.

In conclusion, your new parenting skills should help you prepare to address problem behaviors of your strong-willed child. However, using the parenting skills and maintaining a positive home environment do not guarantee that your child will be problem free. Children will be children and, in particular, strong-willed children will be strong-willed! More realistically, your parenting skills used within a positive climate for behavioral change should reduce the number of behavior problems you have to address. Furthermore, when the problems do arise, you will have the skills to assess and address them. You also will have more opportunity to help your child take advantage of the positive aspects of being strong-willed. You are most likely to achieve these results when you use the parenting skills consistently over time.

PART III

Creating a Strong Foundation for Behavior Change

The five-week program described in Part II for improving your child's strong-willed behavior will be most effective when used in combination with other positive parenting strategies. Since many factors influence children's behavior, behavior management techniques alone are often not enough to drastically change the negative aspects of a child's strong-willed behavior. The parenting techniques presented in Part II will be much more effective when you also provide a stronger foundation for changing your child's behavior. Part III provides our views on how you can change the nature of your family life (Chapter 12), communicate more effectively (Chapter 13), develop greater patience in dealing with your child (Chapter 14), encourage your child's positive self-esteem (Chapter 15), and help improve your child's social skills (Chapter 16).

12

Changing the Nature of Your Family Life

The more positive your family life and the more positively your child views you, the more effectively you will be able to guide your child's behavior and character development. This chapter focuses on ways to make your family life more positive and increase your strong-willed child's chance for success in life. We start by looking at parenting from a historical perspective.

What Can We Learn from Past Generations?

Before the Industrial Revolution, family life in America was very different and, in many ways, more positive than it is today. Although life could be hard, in earlier times, family life was often structured by necessity and involved a great deal of interaction between parents and children. Most young families lived in rural areas near grandparents and other extended family members. Family members typically provided strong support for each other, with many working together on farms or in some type of family activity. Young children spent many hours during the day interacting with their parents and members of the extended family.

Children usually had clearly defined and well-established roles within the family. They were expected to work and make significant contributions to the family at a very young age. Young children helped with cleaning, cooking, and general housekeeping activities. As they became older, children helped in the fields or in some type of activity outside the home. In fact, the two- to three-month summer vacation that children have from school today had its origin in children helping their parents on the farm during growing season. These work activities often involved a great deal of interaction with their parents. Working side-by-side with their parents, children learned not only job skills they would need as they grew up but also a sense of responsibility. Having a meaningful role within the family helped children develop a sense of belonging, self-confidence, and self-discipline.

After working all day together, families typically spent the evenings interacting in other ways. They often used this time for making crafts, telling stories, and relaxing as a family. In other words, family-centered activities were often the focus of free time. The family honored its rituals and traditions, passing them down from generation to generation. Older relatives spent a great deal of time telling stories about the family, which helped impart a sense of belonging and family identity.

In most cases, communities were very close, and community members supported each other, transforming the community into a type of large extended family. In such communities, children typically developed a strong sense of security and belonging, which is the early foundation necessary for the development of positive self-esteem. The importance of community support in rearing children has long been recognized and can be heard in the African proverb "It takes a whole village to raise a child."

In summary, parents and children in the past spent great amounts of time interacting, children had important roles within the family, and extended family members were closely connected to each other, their past, and their community. Through these interactions and life experiences, children learned the life skills and developed the integrity necessary for success.

Positive Homes in Today's Society

Our society has witnessed incredible change over the last fifty years, much of it positive. However, many of the changes have had a negative impact on families and children. Lifestyles that include long working hours outside the home, relocation away from the extended family, family isolation within communities, increased divorce rates, substance abuse, and the prominent role of "screen time" in our lives have made it more difficult for parents and children to interact in ways that prepare children for the world they will be facing. Such changes in our society make it more difficult for children to learn directly from parent-child interactions and from the assumption of meaningful roles within the family, which lead to such positive attributes as respect, responsibility, self-discipline, values, good judgment, perseverance, and self-confidence. As a result, you must plan and work very hard to provide your strong-willed child with the types of interactions and life experiences that will help instill many of the positive attributes once taught as a matter of course.

It is critical that your strong-willed child view his family and home as safe, secure, loving, and enjoyable. To help your child develop positive character and learn important life skills, you must interact with him frequently and positively. Unfortunately, with the pressures of today's society, parents often have great difficulty finding time to spend with their children. Even when we find the time, we often have difficulty putting aside our own concerns and worries so that our time with our children can be really positive. Many of us tend to bring work home. Even if we do not bring home actual work that needs to be completed, we may be so preoccupied with problems at work or other issues in our lives that we cannot really relax and fully enjoy being with our family. When this occurs, it harms your child. If this is a problem for you, you will need to develop strategies for managing the stressful issues in your life (see Chapter 14) so that you can spend more time interacting with your children in a positive way.

Although no home can be totally stress-free, you must make sure that your stress does not "pollute" your home. This pollution can take many forms, including frequent conflict, impatience, anger, withdrawal, moodiness, excessive alcohol use, or drug abuse. Children need a positive and enjoyable home. Your child needs to view you as being in control and being able to handle life's problems. When you can manage the frustrations in your work and home life effectively, you are teaching your child valuable life skills by example. Your child will soon face increasing concerns and worries, and he will have learned from you how to handle stressful situations—whether or not your own skills are good ones.

Unlike parents of past generations who had more time and opportunities to teach their children by example, you must learn how to teach your child important life skills and to build his character with less time and fewer natural opportunities. It is especially important that you make the time and develop the opportunities because, unfortunately, the society in which your child is growing up is filled with violence and uncertainty. In a typical day in the United States, approximately 9 children are killed by firearms, 4,435 are arrested (202 for violent crimes), 2,222 drop out of school, 18,493 are suspended from school, 2,175 are confirmed as abused or neglected, and 1,210 babies are born to teen mothers. Given such statistics, it is easy to see why you must teach your child skills to help him succeed in a society that can be very distressing.

What is the best way to interact with your child to teach him important life skills and develop strong character? Like everyone else, strong-willed children hate being lectured. So just telling him what he needs to know or do *will not be effective*. The most effective way to teach your strong-willed child is by developing a strong relationship with him and then helping him learn through experience and example. The first step in this learning process cannot be overemphasized— develop a strong and positive relationship with your child if you want to have his respect. Unfortunately, children are not born with respect for their parents; it is something that has to be earned. If you have your child's respect and he values his relationship with you, he will want to learn from your example. Simply stated, your child will reflect his environment.

Having Fun Together

One of the ways you can strengthen your relationship with your strong-willed child is to have more fun together. It is important to find activities that you both enjoy. Remember, you, as well as your child, must enjoy the activities. If you are not having fun, the activities will become a chore rather than a means for further developing the positive relationship between you and your child.

It is important that these activities are interactive. In other words, the activities should be things you and your child do together. Some examples of interactive activities are listed in Table 12-1. Having fun is critical, but the ultimate goal is to strengthen your relationship with your child. When people have fun together, they enjoy being with each other and want to spend more time together. The more time people spend interacting in a positive way, the stronger the relationship will become. As you and your child spend more time having fun together, you will develop a greater understanding of each other.

Through fun activities you learn how to cooperate, understand your similarities and differences, and develop respect for each other. You will also gain a greater appreciation of your child's strengths. Interactive activities also allow you the opportunity to nurture his development. This includes providing frequent encouragement and affection. You can help your child develop effective communication skills, social skills, responsibility, values, good judgment, perseverance, self-discipline, and self-confidence. But remember, to be effective in teaching these attributes you must teach through experiences and example, not through lectures. This is one of the most challenging aspects of being an effective parent, and it

Examples of Interactive Activities	**TABLE 12-1**
A collecting hobby (e.g., rocks, sports cards)	Participating in sports
Woodworking	Hiking
Making crafts together	Building models
Going to sports events	Camping
Fishing	Learning magic tricks
Working on art projects	Keeping a family journal
Cooking	Making books (e.g., art, stories, scrapbook)
Gardening and growing vegetables	

requires a lot of time and ingenuity. You will become a stronger role model for him. This is a tremendous responsibility. Your importance as a role model is especially critical during your strong-willed child's early years. When he approaches later childhood and adolescence, your example will be challenged by his peer group and others. You can only hope that the respect you have earned and the example you have provided will have been strong enough to compete with other role models. The importance of trying to impart a sense of morality, responsibility, generosity, empathy, and tolerance during your child's preschool and early school years cannot be overstressed.

The following verse, which is at the entrance to the Louisiana Children's Museum in New Orleans, expresses the importance of teaching your child by having fun through play:

> *I tried to teach my child with books.*
> *He gave me only puzzled looks.*
> *I tried to teach my child with words.*
> *They passed him by often unheard.*
> *Despairingly I turned aside.*
> *"How shall I teach this child?" I cried.*
> *Into my hand he put the key.*
> *"Come," he said, "play with me."*
> *—Author unknown*

The Importance of Play

In this section we discuss the importance of play, especially free play. Play is critical not only for children's cognitive, social, and physical development but also for healthy brain development. For example, researchers have found that active play stimulates brain development, especially in areas of the brain involved in emotion and decision-making skills. Skills learned through play include creativity, critical thinking, spatial skills, and social interaction skills such as sharing and cooperation.

Despite the growing consensus that play is essential for healthy child development, many children have a shrinking amount of time for play. According to Dr. David Elkind of Tufts University, over the past two decades children have lost twelve hours of free time per week, including eight hours per week of unstructured free play and outdoor activities. During this same time period, the amount of time children spend in passive activities has increased approximately 500 percent. The increased time children spend in more passive activities (e.g., watching television, playing video games, and using the computer) is undoubtedly a contributing factor to the current epidemic of childhood obesity.

There are various reasons why we are experiencing a decrease in the amount of time our children have to play. Many preschools and elementary schools are decreasing the amount of time devoted to recess and play due to concerns that children in the United States are falling behind children from other countries academically. As a result of this concern, there has been an increase in time devoted to academic subjects such as math and reading and a decrease in time devoted to recess and physical education. At home, the decreased time available for unstructured play appears to be a result of many factors including our increasingly stressful and hurried lifestyle as well as the increased time devoted to organized sports/activities.

The decreased time available for unstructured child play (play that is not highly directed or controlled by parents or other adults) is especially alarming. There is evidence that suggests young children learn many skills most effectively through active, exploratory play with minimal adult guidance. For example, it is often easier for young children to learn spatial skills through manipulating toys than it is through direct instruction. Children who learn to take things apart, figure out how they work, and how to put them back together often develop strong problem-solving skills. In fact, in his book *Play: How it Shapes the Brain, Opens the Imagination, and Invigorates the Soul*, Dr. Stuart Brown discusses how Cal Tech's Jet Propulsion Laboratory found that the best engineers are not necessarily those who graduated from the most prestigious engineering schools. Rather, they are individuals who as children tended to take things apart and then figure out by themselves how to put them back together. These individuals learned the type of problem-solving skills, through childhood play, that are critical to developing practical solutions to complex problems as engineers.

Given the importance of play, it is critical that you make sure your child has plenty of time for free play. Also make sure that your child has toys and play materials that promote the types of play activities that are most beneficial to your child's development. Below are some suggestions to help you with these recommendations.

- Avoid overscheduling your child with so many activities that he has little time for free play.
- Discourage the overuse of passive entertainment such as television and video games. (Please see Chapter 3 and the later section in this chapter for recommendations on minimizing screen time and maximizing reading.)
- Parents should encourage the use of simple toys (and play materials) that promote creative and imaginative play. Often these types of toys are more "educational" than those that are heavily marketed as educational. Try not to buy toys on impulse or in response to advertisements. Think carefully as to whether the toy will help your child develop important skills such as creativity and problem solving, or allow them the freedom to pretend. Remember that not all children enjoy the same toys or play in the same way. Toys

and play materials that promote skills such as creativity and imagination are listed in the sidebar "Toys and Play Materials That Promote Creative and Imaginative Play."

- Encourage physical play activities that promote physical/motor development and/or exercise. Some toys and activities that promote physical play activities are listed in the sidebar "Toys and Activities That Promote Physical Play."

Most importantly, try not to over-direct or control your child's play. Remember when you were learning the skill of attending in Chapter 6 and we asked you to practice the skill of attending while your child was playing. During these practice sessions, while your child was playing, you were asked to give no instructions, ask no questions, and not use the time to teach your child. These practice-session rules can help you be less controlling of your child's play in general. In our experience, some young children become so dependent on their parent to direct their play activities that it is hard for them to learn how to play independently. So try using these practice session rules (and the skill of attending) to help your child learn to play more independently. When parents take more time to observe their children in play and less time directing their play, they are given a greater opportunity to gain insight into how their child thinks and understands the world.

Minimize Screen Time— Maximize Reading Skills

As we discussed in Chapter 3, most children spend too much time in front of electronic screens (e.g., television, video games, and computer). In addition to the negative effects mentioned in Chapter 3, excessive screen time is also related to decreased reading time and skills necessary to become a good reader. This is important since children who are good readers are more likely to make better grades in school and succeed in life. Children who are good readers also tend to have fewer behavior problems as they get older. So in addi-

Toys and Play Materials That Promote Creative and Imaginative Play

- Blocks
- Dolls
- Dollhouses
- Puppets
- Puppet theater (or a stage made from a big cardboard box to put on puppet shows)
- Finger paints
- Art materials
- Legos (basic building kits offer greater opportunity for creativity than the kits that focus on building specific objects)
- Building sets/materials (e.g., Lincoln Logs, Tinkertoys)
- Sandbox and sandbox toys
- Craft materials
- Modeling clay
- Crayons and blank paper (not just coloring books)
- Play food, utensils, appliances
- Small cars, trucks, trains, airplanes
- Housekeeping toys (e.g., toy vacuums, brooms)
- Storekeeping toys (e.g., cash register, play money, play merchandise)
- Play farm (e.g., animals, barn, fences)
- Box of costumes, hats, and dress-up clothes (let your child put on a "performance" or talent show for you)
- Old sheets and blankets that can be used to build play houses/forts
- Play telephones
- Sidewalk chalk
- A drum set made from pots (or plastic buckets) of different sizes
- A tape recorder for your child to use to record a song or story they make up
- Materials your child can use to make his own book (paper, cardboard covers, binding clips)

tion to reducing your child's screen time (and following the other screen time recommendations we made in Chapter 3), your child will benefit from you focusing on helping him become a good reader.

Toys and Activities That Promote Physical Play

- Balls
- Tricycles/bicycles
- Snow sleds
- Skates
- Jump rope
- Yo-yos
- Flying kites
- Tumbling/gym pad
- Sports equipment
- Hopscotch
- Dancing games
- Playing tag
- Hide-and-seek
- Simon says

The basic skills necessary for your child to become a good reader are acquired before your child ever starts school. For example, children become stronger readers if they start with a foundation of solid language and vocabulary skills. Since parents are their child's first teacher, parents can help teach young children many skills related to later reading ability. Remember not to push too hard. Learning how to read doesn't happen quickly—it takes years. Be patient. It is very important that you make learning how to read fun—not work.

There are many things you can do to prepare your child to eventually become a good reader. The following suggestions can help your child start down the path of becoming someone who loves to read.

- **Help your child develop strong language skills.** Language skills provide the foundation for learning how to read. The first step in helping your child to become a good reader is to focus on verbal/language stimulation.

   —**Talk to your child . . . a lot.** Children learn words more easily and build their vocabulary when they hear them often. A research study found that in the course of daily interactions, young children from high income families heard more than three times as many words per hour as children from low-income families. It is the number of words per hour, not income, that is most important in determining later reading ability.

—**Tell stories.** Children love it when you make up stories that involve them. "Once upon a time, there was a little boy named ___. One day he went to . . ." As your child gets older, he can help you build stories. Start a story and then ask your child what comes next. This kind of dialogue fosters exploration with language and encourages creative thinking. Example: "There was a cat walking along the road . . ." Ask your child, "What happens next?" Allow him to explore options.

—**Label and talk about things in pictures.** Make up stories about pictures. Have your child make up stories from pictures. Encourage the use of descriptive and comparison words.

—**Play word games.** "I spy (with my little eye) something that is (*red*)." "Let's name things that are (*green*). I'm thinking of (*something you would find in a park*)."

• **Read to your child.** Reading to children is the single most powerful thing parents can do at home to help their child become good readers.

—**Read aloud to your child every day.** Make it part of your daily routine. Good times to read to your child often include naptime, bath time, and bedtime.

—**Start with picture books.** Use books that have simple stories and have pictures that will hold your child's attention. Ask your child to help you turn the pages. Read slowly. Use different voices for different characters in the story. Name items in the pictures.

Have your child point to items in the picture ("Can you point to the mouse?").

—**Make reading fun and enjoyable.** Find a comfortable place to read. Have your child sit on your lap or next to you so he can see the printed words and pictures. When you are reading to him, read with a lot of enthusiasm and emotion.

—**Have your child help pick out books for you to read.** Remember that you will get tired of reading the same book over and over long before your child does. It is good for children to hear the same book again and again. He will remember specific words and sentences and have fun saying them with you. Pause in places and have your child finish the sentence from memory.

—**Help your child learn that reading goes from left to right and from top to bottom.** Use your finger to follow the words as you read to your child.

• **Help your child develop a love of books.** Try to help your child develop a lifelong love of books and reading. Make books an important part of your family and home.

—**Visit the library with your child on a regular basis.** Let your child choose (within reason) what books to check out. Let him get his own library card as soon as possible.

—**Help build a book collection for your child.** This doesn't have to cost a lot of money. You can purchase books cheaply at garage sales. Exchange books with other families. Suggest to others that they buy books for your child as presents instead of toys.

—**Let your child see you reading books.** Show him that reading is fun and important. Check out books for yourself when you visit the library with your child. Remember, if your child sees you watching a lot of television, he will want to watch more television. If he sees you reading, he will want to read more.

Making the Most of Household Jobs

Take advantage of various daily activities that provide an opportunity to interact with and teach your child. Although play is important, a great deal of work needs to be done around the home. Let your child help with household jobs as much as possible. Even very young children can help sweep the floor, push the vacuum cleaner, or set the dinner table. Although doing these jobs yourself is often quicker and more practical, involving your child provides a fantastic teaching opportunity. Having your child help with household jobs will give him a sense of contributing to the family and will help him become more responsible and self-confident.

To maintain your strong-willed child's interest in household jobs, you need to offer frequent encouragement and praise. If he is helping you with a task that requires several steps, explain exactly what you are doing step-by-step. For example, when a lightbulb needs changing, first tell your child you need his assistance. This will build his sense of worth within the family. As you go through the steps, talk about each step. This can teach your child not only how to do a specific task but also how to solve problems. You might say the following:

> *Let's take the old lightbulb out of the lamp. You take it out by turning it like this. Do you want to help turn it? Next, we need to check to see what type of bulb it is. See, right here it says "40 watts." Let's go to the kitchen and get a new bulb. See this box? It says "40 watts." That's what we need. You carry the new bulb for me. Let me put it in, and then you can turn it until it is tight and will work. Here, you make it tight by turning it like this. Now turn the light switch on and let's see if it works. Great, we fixed it! Thanks for your help.*

Although this approach takes more time, it is worthwhile. In many ways it is similar to the manner in which parents from past generations taught children to feel a sense of worth within their family. If we always do household jobs ourselves while our children watch television or play video games, how can we expect them to develop a sense of responsibility and a belief that their contribution to the family is important?

Communicating "I Love You"

Most of us don't spend enough time communicating our love to our children (or our spouses). While saying "I love you" is important, there are many other effective ways to communicate your love. Here are just a few ideas:

- Leave little signs with hearts or "I ♥ U" on pieces of paper around the house in places your child will find them (for example, by his bed, on the bathroom mirror, in his coat pocket, in his lunch box).
- Give your child ample physical affection. Hugs can really make children feel loved.
- Let your child overhear you talking to someone else about your love for him. This can be more powerful than telling him directly.
- Start and maintain a family photo album or scrapbook for your child. This lets him know you think he is important and that he is loved. Put selected photographs, artwork, and other information about your child in the album, and let him keep it in his room.
- Give your child a framed photograph of the family to put in his room.
- Display your child's artwork. Don't let him find those valuable masterpieces in the trash.
- Remember that actions speak louder than words.

Be creative! Spend some time generating a list of ways of communicating your love that will be especially meaningful to your child. Every child is different, and developing a personalized list of how to express "I love you" will help you become more aware and responsive to his individuality.

Structure and Routines

A positive home has structure and routines. While too much structure and very rigid routines can be stifling, moderate use of structure and routines can contribute to effective family functioning. Children, especially strong-willed children, need structure. Family rules should be clear and specific (for example, walk—do not run—in the house). Parents should be careful not to have an extremely long list of rules for young children but rather a short list of the most important rules. We recommend having what we refer to as "standing rules," which are "If . . . then" statements. The "If" refers to the prohibited activity. The "then" refers to the consequence for breaking the rule. For example, "*If* you hit your brother, *then* you will go to time-out." Once a standing rule is stated, it is continually in effect. The advantage of having rules specified as "If . . . then" statements is that both the rule and consequence is clearly understood by your child.

It is important to remember that children are creatures of habit who benefit from routines. Routines provide predictable structure that can help guide behavior and improve the emotional climate in the home. A consistent daily routine will help your strong-willed child establish more appropriate behavior. Your child should go to bed at about the same time each night and get up at about the same time every morning. His bedtime routine should be consistent from night to night. The bedtime routine should involve several quieting activities—such as a bath, story, prayer—that occur every night in the same sequence. Morning dressing routines and mealtimes should also be as consistent as possible. Establishing clear and consistent structure and routines in your home can help decrease the amount of time you spend nagging and directing your child.

Family Mealtimes

You may be surprised to learn just how important family meals (when parents and children eat together) are to children's health and well-being. Research indicates that shared family meals are related to improved language development and fewer behavior problems in young children, higher academic achievement of older children, and reduced risk of obesity for all children. When shared family meals continue into the teen years, there is even a relationship to the reduced risk of substance abuse, depression, suicide, and eating disorders.

Although the benefits of family members spending time together during meals is well recognized, the reason why is less well understood. It likely has to do with many factors, including increased family communication (which may strengthen parent-child relationships and stimulate language development in young children as a result of being exposed to more words and interactive dialogue), increased parental presence and supervision of children (parents being more aware of what is going on in their children's lives and at their school), and eating more nutritious meals.

Here are our recommendations for how your child and family can benefit most from family meals.

• **Try to have a minimum of five family meals a week.** (Only 50 to 60 percent of families report eating together at least three to five times per week.) While parent work schedules and children's extracurricular activities can make this very difficult, it is important to make every effort to have as many family meals as possible. Continue frequent family meals as your child gets older.

• **Turn the television off while you are eating.** Almost half of families in the United States have a television in the area where they eat meals. Having the television on during meals appears to disrupt the positive benefits of family mealtimes. For example, when the television is on, there is less family communication and there is a greater likelihood of overeating.

• **Minimize other distractions during family mealtimes.** Turn the radio off. Don't answer the phone or respond to text messages/e-mails. Handheld video games should not be allowed at the table. Keep the focus on the family.

- **Keep mealtime conversations positive and relaxed.** (Don't use the time to focus on problems.) Use mealtimes as a way to catch up on what everyone has done that day and what they have planned for the next day. Use the time to tell family stories. Involve your child in the conversations (be child-focused, not adult-focused). Ideally conversations should involve talking, listening, sharing, caring, and laughing.

- **Consider developing mealtime traditions for your family.** For example, you could play the "question game." Develop a list of questions such as "What is your favorite game?" "What is your favorite joke?" "What was the funniest thing you saw this week?" and place each question on a piece of paper and place all the questions in a jar. Your child gets to pull out a question during certain meals (e.g., dinner on Sunday nights).

- **Keep mealtimes relaxed.** When you have had a stressful day, try to view the family meal as an opportunity to focus on positive things. Try not to let your stress and negative mood carry over to the family meal.

- **Eat at home more.** Meals consumed at home typically include more fruits and vegetables and are lower in calories and fat than restaurant meals.

- **Plan ahead to prepare nutritious meals.** Don't wait until the last minute to decide what to prepare for dinner. When you wait until the last minute, there is a greater tendency to cook packaged processed food or get takeout. Develop a weekly menu and create a shopping list of the items needed.

- **Resist giving in to your child's requests for food items that are not healthy (e.g., sugar-loaded breakfast cereals).** Be aware that children under twelve are the target of almost a billion dollars of food and beverage marketing per year.

- **Teach and expect good manners at the dinner table.** Have clear expectations for mealtime behaviors. Use attending and rewarding to increase good manners (rather than punishing bad manners).

- **Don't make mealtimes too long.** The average mealtime is fifteen to twenty minutes.

Family Traditions and Rituals

Homes feel special and more positive when a family has traditions and rituals. Unfortunately, many parents have not maintained their family's traditions and rituals from past generations. This is a shame since children often love them and they can provide a strong sense of family and family roots. Traditions and rituals help define the uniqueness of a family and help children view their own family as special. Examples of traditions might include a special way for the family to celebrate holidays, such as having a family picnic every Fourth of July, having a family Halloween party every year, or family caroling every Christmas Eve. It is also fun to create unique traditions for your family. For example, you might have small celebrations for children's half-birthdays; when a child turns five and a half, he receives special privileges that day.

We also strongly recommend celebrating a holiday linked to the country of your family's origin. This can be combined with learning more about the country (or countries) of your family's heritage. This is often not only an enjoyable activity but one that teaches children about their family's history. Holiday traditions also can be made special by enjoying unique food, decorations, and activities. Children will often long remember such things as having the holiday meal by candlelight, kissing under the mistletoe, or playing a special game, particularly when such activities occur only on that holiday.

If you want to develop more traditions and rituals for your family, remember to keep them positive and of interest to children and adults alike. The goal is to create activities that your children will not only look forward to but also look back on and cherish when they are adults. Hopefully, these traditions and rituals will be something your children will continue with your grandchildren so that they will be passed on to future generations.

We hope that this chapter has helped you realize the importance of having a positive family environment. As a parent, you play a critical role in laying the foundation for your child learning appropriate behavior and values as well as developing such characteristics as self-confidence, respon-sibility, good judgment, and perseverance. To help your child develop these characteristics, you should increase the positive nature of your family and home. Get more involved with your child, have fun with him, encourage play activities, express your love for him, strengthen relationships within your fam-ily, and teach your child through example. As these efforts help you create a more positive atmosphere for your family, your discipline strategies for behavior problems will become more effective and easier to implement. Perhaps best of all, you will need to use discipline less frequently.

13

Improving Your Communication Skills

Families who communicate effectively tend to have fewer problems, are more likely to address problems successfully when they do arise, and enjoy being with each other more than families who do not communicate effectively. Effective communication skills are a vital building block of successful family functioning. Fortunately, many families demonstrate effective communication patterns. Adults in these families work to communicate what they are thinking and feeling in open and respectful ways. However, even in these families, effective patterns are least likely to be present just when they are needed most—during times of stress. As we discussed in Chapter 3, stress can result from various sources, including financial problems, medical problems, emotional problems, difficulties at work, or parenting a strong-willed child.

The demands placed on a family as a result of having a strong-willed child can add to normal stressors and lead to the development and intensification of breakdowns in communication patterns within the family. Over time, the patterns of poor communication can seriously erode family functioning through a vicious circle in which distress leads to poor communication, poor communication leads to greater distress, greater distress leads to even poorer communication, and so on. The result is that conflict increases and family problems worsen.

Having a strong-willed child influences communication among all family members but may be most detrimental to the communication between parents (whether married or divorced). Parents often end up arguing about discipline at home, problems at child care or preschool, and whom or what to blame for their child's behavior. Over time, the problems and distress that arise from having a strong-willed child influence the communication between parents on issues unrelated to their child. In extreme situations, this vicious circle of poor communication and distress can eventually cause the breakdown of family relationships, as illustrated in the figure "The Strong-Willed Child and the Vicious Cycle of Ineffective Communication Between Parents." To avoid or at least minimize such family crises, parents must actively work on improving their communication skills.

The stress of trying to meet the needs of a strong-willed child can eventually cause communication breakdowns between parents and others who care for or interact with the child, including relatives, child care workers, and teachers. Therefore, even in single-parent families in which the non-custodial parent has minimal or no involvement in child rearing, the parent who is with the child can benefit from trying to improve his or her communication skills.

Communication Problems and Solutions

In this chapter, we present some common communication problems and recommend solutions to those problems. Changing communication styles can be very difficult, so it will require a major effort. Old habits are hard to break! We recommend identifying only one or two communication problems to work on at a time. Let your partner or a significant other know specifically what skills you are going to work on. Ask your partner to help point out to you (very gently!) when you err and to offer positive feedback as you make progress. This process typically works best when your partner is also

The Strong-Willed Child and the Vicious Cycle of Ineffective Communication Between Parents

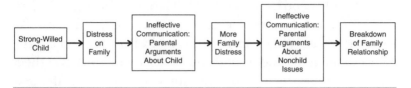

trying to improve communication because the two of you can support each other. A supportive atmosphere is essential to effectively change communication patterns. An atmosphere of criticism and finger-pointing will inevitably cause your efforts to fail.

Problem #1: Inattention

Most people would agree that you cannot have a meaningful conversation if one person is not paying attention to what the other person is saying. Although we all recognize the importance of attending to what is being said, inattention is the most common communication problem. Inattention can result from various external and internal factors. External factors include distractions such as interruptions by children, a phone ringing, or a loud television. Internal factors that prevent us from paying attention include fatigue, anger, anxiety, thoughts about something else that is pressing (such as being late for an appointment), or general indifference to what the other person has to say.

Inattention to what another person is saying is easy to recognize if you observe the conversation, specifically watching body language. People who are not really listening are often looking away from the person speaking or are making negative facial expressions such as sneers, smirks, glares, or looks of disgust. Inattention is also obvious from the verbal content of conversations. Conversations marked by inattention typically involve frequent interruptions in order to question, argue, or criticize. It is hard to feel that someone is listening to you when he or she repeatedly interrupts you!

Solution: Be an Effective Listener

Being a truly good listener is hard. It can require a lot of effort and practice! However, the payoff for becoming a good listener makes it well worth the effort. Most people can accept differing opinions and disagreements as long as they feel their perspective has been heard and understood. Since effective listening is considered to be the most important communication skill, we are devoting more attention to listening than to some of the other communication skills. To be an effective listener, you should develop a listening style that incorporates the following good practices.

Eliminate Distractions. When you make the effort to do this, you show the person who is talking to you that you are interested in what he or she is saying. So, turn off the television (or at least turn down the volume), put down the newspaper, and eliminate other distractions. If you cannot eliminate distractions immediately, indicate that you really want to hear what your partner has to say. Suggest another time (such as when the children are outside playing) when you will be able to discuss the issue without interruption.

Listen to Understand. When people are discussing an issue, they sometimes have already made up their minds about it. When this happens, they probably do not really listen to the other person, which can be very frustrating. When this type of communication pattern occurs frequently, it can be devastating to a relationship. Instead, make the effort to really listen to understand what your partner is saying. Simply stated, listen for content. Try to separate *what* is being said from *how* it is said. Try to understand the issue from your partner's perspective. Of course, you have the right to disagree, but express your thoughts only after your partner has expressed his or her views. Remember, people are much more likely to respect your disagreement if they feel that you have really listened to and tried to understand their perspective.

Reflect and Summarize What You Hear. How can you let your partner know that you have really listened and tried to understand what he or she is saying? A useful way to do this is through reflection and summarization. *Reflection* refers to making comments during the course of a conversation that indicate you are really paying attention to what is being said. The father in the following conversation uses reflection very effectively:

> *Mother: I feel like I'm at the end of my rope. Jonathan's behavior is driving me crazy. He is constantly trying to get my attention, and he will not stop whining. It's "Mommy, do this" and "Mommy, do that" all day long. I feel like I spend all day waiting on him.*
> *Father: It must be so frustrating having to deal with him all day without a break.*

Another type of response that indicates attention, *summarizing*, involves stating *in a nonjudgmental way* the overall point the other person is making. It is particularly useful when discussing complex issues or after a lengthy discussion. Let's look at an example:

> *Father: Jonathan's preschool teacher called me at work today to say that Jonathan has been getting into a lot of trouble at school. She said the problems start as soon as he arrives and starts playing with Matthew. When Matthew doesn't do what he wants him to, Jonathan starts calling him names and even pushes and hits him. At snack time he often tries to take Matthew's snack away from him. At recess he pushes Matthew around on the playground. What really worries me is that she said the preschool cannot tolerate aggressive behavior. I don't know what we would do if they ever did kick him out.*

> Mother: *Well, it seems as if the major problem is between Jonathan and Matthew since the teacher didn't say anything about problems with other children. We need to think about what things we can do to address the problem.*

Jonathan's mother did a nice job of summarizing a lengthy, and probably emotional, dialogue by her husband about a complicated issue. Her statement assured her husband that she was listening. Furthermore, she was able to propose an initial plan of action for the problem.

Clarify to Reach Full Understanding. When you clarify, or ask pertinent questions about what another person is saying, you increase your understanding of his or her perspective, as well as indicate that you are listening. In clarifying, you express interest in trying to fully understand what the other person is saying. Although most of us ask questions for clarification in our jobs and other activities, we are much less likely to do so in our personal relationships, especially when conversations involve stressful family issues. However, the discussion of stressful family issues is perhaps the most important time to ask clarifying questions.

Use Receptive Body Language. Your body language can tell a great deal about how interested you are in what another person is saying. You clearly communicate your lack of interest in what is being said when you do not look at the person who is talking. When you look away, continue to read the newspaper, or watch television when your partner is talking to you, you send a strong message: what you are hearing is not important. You also express lack of interest when you mimic or make faces at your partner as he or she is talking.

When you express disinterest and disrespect in such ways, the conversation more than likely turns to conflict or simply ends. Some ways of expressing interest through body language include maintaining eye contact, facing your partner, projecting a facial expression of interest, nodding occasionally to demonstrate that you agree with certain things that are being said, and avoiding negative facial expressions (or other negative gestures). The nonverbal message you want to convey is "I respect you enough to listen and try to understand your perspective."

Problem #2: Monopolizing the Conversation

It is hard to carry on a real conversation when one person monopolizes it. We have all tried to have conversations in which the other person would not let us get a word in edgewise. A dominant talker may be fine in certain social conversations, but this behavior presents a problem when two people are discussing an issue of importance to both of them. If you monopolize conversations and are only interested in gaining support for your own views and opinions, your partner will probably begin to feel resentful, and his or her frustration will build. At this point, your partner is likely to become angry, and communication probably will break down.

It is important to note that a parent who consistently monopolizes conversations is modeling for her child exactly what we want the child to avoid doing. (Review Chapter 2 for a discussion of the importance of modeling in parenting.) Instead we, as parents, want to provide our child with an example of balanced communication, with as much (if not more) emphasis on listening as talking. This is best taught by parental modeling. As a reminder, children learn best by what we do, not what we tell them to do.

Solution: Request Feedback and Take Turns Talking

Individuals who monopolize conversations tend to be more extroverted and talkative. If you are a "talker" and monopolize conversations, you may need to take steps to involve others more. This is especially true when you are talking to someone who tends to be quiet and introverted and who may be reluctant to interrupt you in an effort to express his or her views and opinions.

When you are discussing an issue with your partner, make a point to ask for his or her opinions and views. In doing so, avoid questions that encourage simple yes-or-no answers. For example, saying, "You agree with me, don't you?" encourages the other person to simply say "Yes." These types of questions are called *closed-ended questions* as they often close the line of communication. Instead, try to ask questions that promote dialogue. Questions that promote conversations begin with the words *how, when, what,* or *why.* Such questions are commonly referred to as *open-ended questions.* These questions encourage the other person to express his or her views or opinions and open up the line of communication. For example, "What happened at work today?" will promote more conversation than the yes-or-no response you are likely to receive from a closed-ended question such as "Did you have a good day at work?" Again, when our children see us use this type of open communication style, they are more likely to use it themselves.

Problem #3: Silence

On the opposite extreme from people who monopolize conversations are those who remain silent. Many of these people try to avoid conflict or disapproval by keeping thoughts and feelings to themselves during discussion. Not speaking does avoid conflict and disapproval in the short run. However, if you let feelings bottle up inside you, you are likely to reach a point at which you explode in anger. This certainly does not improve communication!

Solution: Speak Up

You can avoid angry outbursts from bottled-up feelings by expressing your feelings and opinions as they arise during conversations. This is difficult for many people. If you are someone for whom speaking up does not come naturally, you will have to plan how to speak up before you actually can do it. Here is a plan for learning how to speak up in conversations:

- Think about the worst thing that can happen if you speak your opinion. It rarely is horrible.
- Think about the good things that can happen if you express your opinion. These include modeling effective communication and prevention of bottled-up feelings.
- Plan to express your opinion in a conversation with one particular person, ideally someone who is likely to be supportive.
- Do it and evaluate the consequences. They will not be as bad as you think.

Problem #4: Being Judgmental

Many of us have very strong opinions about numerous issues. If you are one of these people, your partner may be reluctant to express differing views. Your partner may believe you are not open to considering other views and will judge him or her negatively. In such situations, your partner often withdraws from the conversation. As a result, resentment builds over time. This does not help the relationship or the development of effective communication between the two of you.

Solution: Express Openness to Listen to Other Views

Although you may have strong opinions regarding certain issues, demonstrate a willingness to hear other opinions. This does not mean that you are going to change your opinions, just that you are willing to listen to opposing viewpoints. Avoid putting down your partner when he or she expresses a differing opinion. Discuss the concerns you have about the idea rather than attacking your partner as a person. When listening to other perspectives, try to keep an open mind as much as possible. At some later point, on some issue, your partner may convince you that he or she is right!

Problem #5: Dwelling on Past Problems During Conflicts

When we are discussing a conflict, some of us tend to bring up past conflicts. For example, you might catch yourself saying, "It's just like when you . . ." When you do this repeatedly, it makes your partner feel as if he or she will never be forgiven for past transgressions or allowed to change. This can lead to negative feelings and to a breakdown in communication.

Solution: Stick to the Present Issue

When discussing problems, try to focus on the problem at hand. Avoid bringing up past problems that are not directly related to the present. For a relationship to flourish, the people involved must be willing to focus forward and to forgive, if necessary. We all make mistakes. Hopefully, we can learn from them without having to be repeatedly reminded about them. Try to be forgiving and live in the present. This is a valuable lesson to teach our children. Mistakes are opportunities to learn, and we, as parents, will teach our children that this lesson is true by our own example—as we focus on the present.

Problem #6: Focusing on Who Is to Blame

In our society, we often want to focus on who is to blame for a problem. This concern with assigning blame occurs at the national, local, and family levels. However, whether the problem is the federal budget deficit or a child's behavior, most major problems are the result of several factors, not just one. Trying to identify or focus on who is to blame is rarely productive. Finger-pointing usually leads to hurt feelings, not solutions to a problem.

Solution: Focus on Developing Solutions to Problems

Rather than assessing blame for a problem, it is much more effective to focus on potential solutions for the problem. For instance, if four-year-old Richard has been heard using foul language repeatedly, it will be much more productive for his parents to focus on developing a united approach for dealing with the problem rather than blaming each other for the times they have each used foul language in Richard's presence. In such cases, it is certainly acceptable to discuss factors that may be playing a role, such as overhearing others using foul language, as long as the focus is on identifying solutions, such as not modeling use of foul language, rather than finger-pointing. Because most problems, including those related to a child's behavior, result from many factors, the answer is rarely simple. Placing blame will not solve the problem.

Problem #7: Cross-Complaining

When someone complains about something you have done, a common reaction is to respond by complaining about something that person has done. For example, if you complain about your spouse's lack of help with the housework, your spouse may complain about your lack of affection. The philosophy behind such cross-complaining is that the best defense is a good offense. That is, the way to protect myself when verbally attacked is to counterattack. Unfortunately, instead of solving a problem, cross-complaining often escalates into an argument.

Solution: Work on the Current Issue

It is hard to accept another person's complaint about you or your behavior without getting at least somewhat upset. Still, try to rise above your initial emotional reaction, and resist the temptation to lash back. If you can avoid the trap of cross-complaining and instead focus on the issue at hand, you have a much better chance of successfully addressing the current problem. If you disagree with what your partner is saying, discuss the issue from a problem-solving perspective. Try to understand the complaint from your partner's point of view. Listen to exactly what your partner is saying and ask yourself why he or she is saying it. Is there any truth in it? Discuss what *each* of you can do to avoid the same problem in the future.

Problem #8: Mind Reading

At times, many of us assume we know what another person is thinking. Assumptions are especially likely among people who know each other well. If you start assuming you know what your partner is thinking, you are heading down a dangerous path. If you have not asked, you will never know for sure. When you say, "I know what you're thinking," or "I know you think . . . ," it puts your partner on the defensive. Over time, a lot of resentment can develop if you are repeatedly speaking your partner's mind.

Solution: Speak Only for Yourself

During conversations, especially those that involve some level of conflict, speak only for yourself. Let your partner express his or her own opinions. You also may want to encourage your partner to express his or her opinions by asking what he or she thinks. Avoid interrupting when he or she begins to speak. Do not assume you know what your partner is thinking and is about to say!

Problem #9: Disrespect and Put-Downs

Unfortunately, people tend to show less respect for loved ones than for casual acquaintances. Most of us are generally polite and respectful toward people we do not know very well. However, knowing someone well sometimes makes you feel as if you have permission to be less than respectful. This disrespect often includes using put-downs such as "You're lazy," "You're stupid," or even "You're worthless." These are hurtful words that chip away at a relationship.

Solution: Be Polite and Use "I" Messages

If you treat the people you love with respect, you will greatly reduce the amount of conflict in your relationships. Make every effort to be as polite to those you love as you are to others. Try to express yourself rather than just vent your feelings. When you find yourself about to say something that could be a put-down to your partner, rethink the words you are about to use and present the message in a less threatening way. How can you do this?

It is more effective to describe how you feel about a problem than to hurl accusations. Describing how you feel is often referred to as the use of *"I" messages*—that is, statements about yourself that begin with the word *I*. These types of messages communicate your feelings or needs. *"You" messages*, on the other hand, are about the person you are talking to—they begin with the word *you*. Such statements often direct blame or criticism at the other person. Let's look at an example of these two types of messages:

"You" message	"You are such a slob. You just throw your stuff all over the place, and you never help clean up."
"I" message	"I get so frustrated about the house being such a mess. I feel like I constantly need to clean up, but I just don't have the time to do it myself. I really need some help."

Think about how much more willing you would be to help clean up after hearing the "I" message than the "you" message. Although "I" messages cannot solve all communication problems, they can minimize conflict and encourage healthier patterns of communication.

Problem #10: Mixed Messages

Imagine your spouse tells you he or she is interested in what you have to say but does not look at you when you are talking. Your spouse's behavior is inconsistent with his or her words. When verbal and nonverbal messages conflict in this way, what message do you choose to receive? Mixed messages can be hard, if not impossible, to interpret.

Research suggests that people will give at least as much weight to your nonverbal messages as to your verbal ones. Renowned psychologist Albert Mehrabian found that only 7 percent of what we communicate is done through words; 38 percent is through nonverbal vocal characteristics such as tone and volume, and 55 percent is through body movements such as facial expressions. Regardless of the exact percentages, it is well documented that nonverbal communication is very important.

Solution: Use Consistent Verbal and Nonverbal Messages

To be understood correctly, make sure your verbal and nonverbal messages are in sync. For example, if you are saying something positive, your nonverbal language also needs to be positive. Positive nonverbal language includes facial expressions (such as smiling and looking empathetic), body language (such as touching or leaning toward the person), and tone of voice (for example, warm, joyful, caring, or happy).

Putting Solutions into Action

As we mentioned at the beginning of this chapter, changing your patterns of communication is often very difficult. To give you a handy reference, Table 13-1 summarizes the ten communication problems and solutions we have discussed. Review them and decide which areas are problems for you. Also, get feedback from others. One way to do this is to ask your spouse or a friend to indicate which of the solutions in

Review of Communication Problems and Solutions	TABLE 13-1
Problem	**Solution**
Inattention	Be an effective listener.
Monopolizing the conversation	Request feedback and take turns talking.
Silence	Speak up.
Being judgmental	Express openness to listen to other views.
Dwelling on past problems during conflicts	Stick to the present issue.
Focusing on who is to blame	Focus on developing solutions to problems.
Cross-complaining	Work on one problem at a time.
Mind reading	Speak only for yourself.
Disrespect and put-downs	Be polite and use "I" messages.
Mixed messages	Use consistent verbal and nonverbal messages.

this chapter are strengths they have observed in you. You then may assume that the other areas are the ones on which you should focus.

After identifying specific problems and potential solutions, you may need to establish a structured approach to learn how to use the solutions. This approach might include practicing with a tape recorder or video camera, role-playing with someone, or using planned discussions. Planned discussions involve selecting a time and place free from distraction where you can discuss specific issues with your spouse or close friend in order to practice the communication skills you are trying to master. For some suggestions of communication builders to incorporate in your planned discussions, see "Does Your Communication Style Need Improvement?" Try to apply these tips to all of your conversations!

Does Your Communication Style Need Improvement?

Nobody is perfect, and that axiom applies to communication as well as to the other things we do. But there are some communication styles that can really turn people off. Pay attention to the way you talk to others this week. How often do you hear yourself using some of these negative communication styles?

- Nagging
- Lecturing
- Interrupting
- Criticizing
- Sarcasm
- Threatening

If you use some of these negative practices, work on improving your communication style. Focus on replacing the negatives with some of these communication builders:

- Be clear and specific in what you say.
- Use "I" messages.
- Ask for feedback about what you are saying.
- Focus on positives.
- Ask questions that promote detailed responses:
  "I'd really like to hear about . . ."
  "Can you tell me more?"
  "What do you think about . . . ?"
  "Can you explain that to me?"

Being an effective communicator is difficult, but if you learn the skills presented in this chapter, you can improve your communication style. These skills will also indirectly improve the behavior of your strong-willed child because you will communicate more effectively with your child and will be more effective in discussing your concerns about him with others. Providing a positive communication model is a gift to our children that can last a lifetime!

14

Developing More Patience

Parents of strong-willed children often report that their patience is constantly tested. They have to deal not only with the typical stressors of parenthood but also with a child who can be very demanding. The constant demands would take their toll on almost any parent's patience! Therefore, it is normal to sometimes lose your patience and feel upset, frustrated, or angry.

Unfortunately, being the parent of a strong-willed child places you in a difficult dilemma. Your child's demanding behavior increases the chance that you will lose your patience, but your child needs you to be patient *more* than most other children do. Strong-willed children respond best to parents who can handle problems in a matter-of-fact way. When you lose your patience, you lose control of effectively managing your child's behavior.

Losing your patience, especially if it happens often, can create significant problems in the long run, even if it sometimes appears to have remedied the situation in the short term. The more patient you can be, especially in the face of your child's disruptive behavior, the more effective you will be as a parent. However, as you well know, this is not easy.

In this chapter we will discuss the relationship between how you think about your child's behavior and how patient you are. Understanding this strong relationship will help you learn to become more patient and thus be a more effective parent. After discussing this relationship, we will present ways to improve your patience by changing how you think. Unfortunately, even after learning ways to increase your patience, you probably will lose your patience again at some point. Therefore, we also will discuss what can you do when you feel you're at the end of your patience. Finally, because people lose patience more often when they become stressed, we will conclude the chapter with general strategies to minimize the negative effects of stress in your life.

Patience and the Way You Think

When you are with your child, you probably experience a wide range of emotions. Some are good; some are not so good. Most parents think those feelings are caused by their child's behavior. Suppose your child has a temper tantrum in a store, and you become upset. You might conclude that the temper tantrum caused you to become upset. However, his temper tantrum does not *directly* cause you to become upset. What causes you to become upset is the way you view the temper tantrum.

Let's look at some different ways you might view your child's tantrum. If your child begins a temper tantrum in public and you think that he should always behave himself in public, you might view him as bad or mean, which may lead you to become angry and start yelling at him. Or you might start thinking that others view you as a terrible mother for not being able to control your child. In this case, you might question your ability to be a good parent, start feeling depressed, and do nothing to address his tantrum because you lack the confidence to take action. A third, and more appropriate, view may be that the tantrum resulted from his being overtired and needing a nap. In this case, you would probably not become very upset but rather decide that it is time to go home so that he can take his nap.

The Cause of Parents' Emotional Reactions

Your child's behavior *does not* directly cause your emotional reaction.

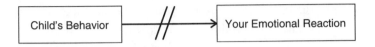

Your emotional reaction depends on how you think about your child's behavior.

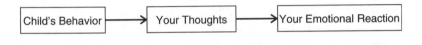

As in this example, your child's behavior itself does not make you become upset or lose your patience. You cause yourself to lose your patience by the way you view his behavior. See the figure "The Cause of Parents' Emotional Reactions," which illustrates this important point.

Certain common ways of thinking about a child's behavior often lead parents to lose their patience:

- "My child should never behave in certain ways."
- "I am a bad parent if my child behaves in certain ways."
- "It is terrible, and I can't stand it when my child behaves in certain ways."
- "My child behaves in certain ways to make me suffer."
- "My child should always behave well."
- "My child is always trying to get on my nerves."
- "I need to get angry to correct my child's behavior."

Becoming aware of these thoughts will allow you to identify whether you have similar thoughts, which put you at risk for more easily losing your patience with your child. If you identify with these thoughts, you should pay special attention to the next section.

Changing Your Negative Thoughts

All children are going to misbehave at times or do things that their parents do not like. Therefore, it is not terrible or awful when your child misbehaves unless you convince yourself that it is terrible or awful. This does not mean that you should be content with or condone your child's misbehavior. However, you do need to have a realistic perspective regarding your child's behavior, and you need to avoid negative absolute thinking.

Negative absolute thinking occurs when you start thinking negatively in absolute ways about something and use terms that include *should, must,* or *always.* For example, you might think, "My child should never misbehave." But, all children are going to misbehave. If you think your child should never misbehave, you are setting yourself up to lose your patience and become angry when he does.

Many parents think in negative absolute terms. If you are one of these parents, try to challenge and change those thoughts. For example, if you tend to think that your child should never misbehave, try to think along more reasonable lines when he does misbehave. You might say to yourself, "I don't like it when he behaves like this, but I can handle it." Also, try to be realistic and acknowledge to yourself that all children misbehave and it is not terrible when your child misbehaves. You do not have to like it, but admit that it is going to happen and that it is undesirable—not terrible. *Terrible* is when your child is stricken with a life-threatening illness, not when he has a temper tantrum at the shopping mall!

Let's look at another common way of thinking in negative absolute terms: thinking other people believe you are a bad parent when your child misbehaves. If you have such a thought, try to challenge it. A more realistic thought is that most parents have had similar experiences and probably empathize with you in such a situation. Even if they do not understand, you do not need the approval of strangers to know that you are a good parent and you are doing the best you can with a difficult, strong-willed child. Try to replace your negative absolute thinking with these more realistic thoughts. After all, your worth as a parent is not based on your child's behavior in public places!

Some parents who are prone to negative absolute thoughts find it helpful to consciously start reciting more realistic and helpful thoughts to themselves when their children misbehave. Here are some sample statements:

- "My child will misbehave sometimes even when he knows the rules."
- "When my child misbehaves, all he has done is broken a rule."
- "Getting angry will not help me effectively deal with my child."
- "It is undesirable and irritating when my child misbehaves, but it is not terrible."
- "I can handle this situation more effectively if I stay calm."
- "I am not a bad parent just because my child broke a rule. All children break rules."

This realistic self-talk helps avoid the trap of thinking negatively out of habit.

Another kind of negative thinking involves making negative assumptions about the intentions of your child's behavior. An example is assuming your child is misbehaving to get back at you for something you did. Although this may occasionally be the case, young children rarely misbehave in order to get revenge or to get on your nerves. However, when you make such an assumption, you are more likely to lose patience.

Try not to assume the worst. In most cases, young children misbehave to get something they want or to avoid something they do not want to do. Their motives are typically self-centered and do not include a desire to upset their parents. This may be hard to believe at times, but it is true!

What to Do When You Lose Your Patience

Almost all parents lose their patience at times. Even if you try really hard to change your negative thoughts, you are likely at some time to lose your patience and become angry. If you think in absolute terms that you should never lose your patience, that you should always be patient, and that it is terrible if you lose your patience, you may very well become upset or depressed when you do.

Becoming upset or depressed when you lose your patience will not help you be more patient in the future. Instead, when you lose your patience, acknowledge that it is undesirable and unfortunate but also human. Expecting yourself to always be patient is unrealistic. Do not make excuses for losing your patience, but instead acknowledge and understand that it is going to happen on occasion.

Since you probably will lose your patience with your child in the future, what can you do to minimize the negative effects? We recommend using the four Rs of damage control:

1. *Recognize* that you have lost your patience.
2. *Remove* yourself or step back from the situation.
3. *Review* the situation.
4. *Respond* to the situation.

The first step is to *recognize* as soon as possible that you have lost your patience. Since we all react somewhat differently, try to identify your personal signals that indicate you are losing or have lost your patience. Examples of such signals might be a hot flash, a clenched jaw, a clenched fist, a pounding heart, swearing, or starting to raise your voice. The key is to identify that you are losing (or have lost) your patience as early as possible so that you can regain control of yourself more easily.

The second step is to *remove* yourself from the situation as soon as you recognize that you are losing or have lost your patience. If you are at home or in public with another adult who can assume temporary responsibility for your child, walking away for a few moments may be most effective. Of course, no matter how mad you are, you should never leave your young child unattended in a potentially dangerous situation, such as alone in a public place. When you cannot physically leave the situation, try to step back—literally. Take a couple of steps away from your child, look at something other than your child, and try to regain your composure. Take some deep breaths and try to calm yourself as much as possible. Recite to yourself realistic thoughts about your child's behavior, such as the ones suggested earlier. For example, say to yourself, "My child broke a rule. Getting angry and losing control will not help me effectively deal with this situation." This type of positive self-talk can be very effective in managing anger and regaining self-control.

Once you have gained your self-control, pause and briefly *review* the situation to yourself. Think about what happened, how your thoughts led you to lose your patience, and how you can best handle the present situation. Then decide on what you think is the most effective response.

The final step is to confront the situation and *respond* in the way you have decided is most appropriate. Maintain your self-control while you are responding to the situation. If you sense that you are losing your patience again, start back at the beginning and go through the four Rs again: *recognize*, *remove yourself*, *review*, and *respond*.

Try to move through the four Rs as quickly as possible. When you remove yourself and review the situation, do not become caught up in all the details of the situation or all the possible ways of responding. If you take too long reviewing the situation, you may lose your chance to respond most effectively. After the situation has resolved, you can analyze it in greater detail and think about possible responses that you did not consider initially. Analyzing the situation later, when you are more relaxed, can lead to more creative ideas that might be helpful the next time you are confronted with a similar situation. At this time, ask yourself, "What do I like about the way I handled that situation?" and "What would I do differently next time?"

Managing the Stress in Your Life

Along with your thoughts about your child's behavior, other factors also influence your level of patience. Most of these are sources of stress. The more stressed you are, the less patient you will be. If you can reduce your stress or manage it more effectively, you will reduce the probability that you will lose your patience. A number of general strategies can help you manage the stress most adults experience.

Identify and Reduce Stressors

Unfortunately, we cannot eliminate many of the stressors in our lives. We must usually accept and work around stress factors such as health problems and job responsibilities. However, if you are like most people, there are probably numerous small stressors in your life that you can eliminate or reduce.

The first step is to identify what contributes to your stress. Make a list of all the stressors, big and small, that affect you. Then go through the list and mark the stressors that you can change or eliminate. For instance, some people become stressed by overcommitting themselves. If this is true for you, resolve to start being more assertive and reducing your commitments.

Keep in mind that not only the "big" things, like finances, cause stress. For some people, the daily hassles of life build up to cause the most stress. If this is the case for you, try to minimize the small hassles. Organization is the key. Try to plan out each day. For example, by developing a daily plan, you may be able to do all your errands in one trip rather than two or three. This can be a big time-saver and reduce stress.

In sum, the initial step is to identify the stressors you can change. The next step is to decide exactly what changes to make. Then do it!

Take a Break or Change Gears

If you were to list the most stressful occupations, you might list jobs like police officer, firefighter, or doctor. While these occupations are stressful, the people doing these jobs have time away from work to recuperate. They rarely work twenty-four hours a day, and if they do, they usually have periods of time off from work to recover.

Now, think about being a parent—especially the parent of a strong-willed child—and remember that the small stressors of life often have the biggest impact, which is especially true when we have little relief from these ongoing small stressors. From this perspective, being a parent is one of the most stressful jobs in the world. We are parents twenty-four hours a day, seven days a week. Many parents of young children have little time off from the daily hassles of being a parent.

As the parent of a strong-willed child, you therefore need to take breaks from your parenting role. How you do this can vary greatly. Regardless of how you do it, the main goal should be for you to spend at least several hours a week doing something you really enjoy. Your activity might be something you consider relaxing, such as taking a nap, reading, going to a movie, or being with friends. Other kinds of breaks also can be helpful. For some people, just changing gears and doing something different from the routine of parenting is most helpful. For example, volunteer work outside the home is one way to change gears. The point is to do something that you enjoy doing so that you can have a regular break or change of pace from the daily demands and hassles of parenting.

Learn How to Relax

When most people become really stressed, they show signs of physical tension. Common symptoms are tense muscles, headaches, rapid and shallow breathing, and increased blood pressure. One way of managing stress is learning how to relax in order to reduce such physical tension.

Sample Relaxation Exercise

The technique described here involves visualization and breathing exercises. This brief description alone cannot provide you with the skills necessary to achieve the level of relaxation necessary to significantly reduce your physical tension. However, we hope it will give you an idea of what relaxation training can involve.

Before practicing this technique, lie down or sit in a comfortable chair that offers support for your head. Eliminate distractions by turning off the television, radio, computer, and all cell phones. Then choose a location and time you will not be disturbed.

Start by placing yourself in a comfortable position where all parts of your body, including your legs, arms, and head, are supported. Keep your legs uncrossed. Close your eyes. Try to focus initially on blocking out all other thoughts and concentrate solely on your breathing. Slow down your breathing. Take deep, relaxing breaths. Make your breathing smooth; that is, breathe in slowly and out slowly. Try to create a smooth rhythm to your breathing. Try to block out all other thoughts and concentrate solely on your breathing.

After your breathing becomes relaxed and rhythmic, imagine a small amount of tension in your body leaving through your breath each time you exhale. Imagine the tension being sucked out of your body each time you exhale. Imagine the tension leaving your feet, legs, back, shoulders, neck, and elsewhere in your body. Each time you inhale, imagine a small wave of relaxation spreading throughout your body from your head to your toes.

Try to continue this exercise for several minutes. Then daydream about a relaxing situation. For some people, it might be lying on the beach, or for others, lying in a field looking up at the clouds. The exact scene is unimportant as long as it is relaxing to you. (You should decide on the scene before beginning the relaxation exercise so you do not have to waste time and energy deciding on a scene when you are relaxed.) The most important thing to remember as you are daydreaming about your scene is to try to involve all your senses. Imagine that you are really there. Imagine not only the visual aspects of the scene but also the sounds, smells, and sensations. For example, if you imagine yourself at the beach, imagine the sounds of the surf, the birds, and the children playing in the distance. Imagine the smells of saltwater and perhaps suntan lotion. Also imagine the sensation of the sun's warmth on your skin and the feeling of the wind as it blows across your body. Try to actually put yourself at the beach mentally.

After you have practiced daydreaming for at least five to ten minutes, you can slowly open your eyes and focus on how relaxed you feel.

You can use such relaxation exercises as brief respites from the daily stressors in your life. They can be viewed as brief catnaps that relax and refresh your body. Over time, and with training, many people learn how to use such techniques to quickly put themselves in a relaxed state during times of tension.

Many people believe they already know how to relax. However, effective relaxation is more than just sitting down in front of the television, taking a coffee break, or having a beer or glass of wine with friends. These activities may distract a person from stress or help the person cope, but they generally do not reduce physical tension.

One effective technique for combating physical tension is to learn and practice specific relaxation exercises (see the box "Sample Relaxation Exercise"). There are many types of relaxation exercises. Some involve learning to tense and relax specific muscle groups, while others involve breathing and visualization techniques. For these relaxation exercises to be most effective in reducing physical tension, you must practice them daily.

There are many ways to learn relaxation techniques. Mental health professionals often teach them individually. Your local hospital, community college, or other organization may offer classes in relaxation or stress management. Or you can learn on your own with one of the many books and audiotapes or CDs on the subject that you can purchase at a bookstore or online.

Learn Effective Problem-Solving Strategies

Problems in our lives, whether at work or at home, can cause stress. They can cause extreme stress when we do not know how we should handle them and, as a result, become overwhelmed. You are less likely to feel overwhelmed if you learn and practice a strategy for solving problems. One problem-solving process involves the following steps:

1. Try to relax and remain calm.
2. Clearly define the specific problem.
3. Generate a list of possible solutions.
4. Evaluate the solutions on the list.
5. Choose what you think is the best solution.
6. Implement the solution and evaluate the outcome.

To use this problem-solving process effectively, try to remain relaxed. The more tense and upset you become, the less clearly you will think, and the less effectively you will address the problem. When you are calm, try to clearly define the problem. Many times we do not effectively address problems because we look only at the symptoms instead of defining the exact problem. Once you have specifically defined the problem, generate a list of possible solutions. At this stage, do not think about whether each is a good or bad solution or even if it is realistic. You just want to brainstorm and come up with as many potential solutions as possible.

After you have exhausted your thoughts on potential solutions, it is time to evaluate the solutions on your list. Review each potential solution and decide whether it is at all possible and whether it would produce the desired result. Also think about the negative repercussions of each solution. After evaluating all the possible solutions, choose the solution that you think is best, all factors considered. Some people never can make a decision because none of the options is ideal. If you are one of these people, remind yourself that most problems do not have an ideal solution (just as there are no ideal children!) and that you must choose the best possible solution for you. Typically, if you fail to select and implement a solution, you perpetuate stress. Finally, at some point after implementing the solution you selected, evaluate the outcome and how you did in making the decision. Make sure you praise yourself if the solution you selected was a good one. If the selected solution was not a good one, use the experience as a time of learning. Think about other solutions that might have been more effective.

Get Enough Rest

Everyone is tired at times, but frequently or constantly feeling tired is a problem. If you are like most people, you have less patience when you are tired. You may have difficulty seeing things objectively and using problem-solving skills. You may have a greater tendency to overreact to certain situations. Being tired creates problems that result in even more stress. If stress is a problem for you, you must get enough rest to effectively deal with the stressful situations you face.

Try to establish a consistent bedtime that will allow you to sleep sufficiently. Staying up past midnight every night and rising at 6:00 A.M. allows too little sleep time for most people. In the end, you will be able to achieve more (especially in terms of quality) if you have enough rest than if you regularly stay up late to complete things. One way to do this is to have consistent times for going to bed and rising.

If you have difficulty falling asleep, you might want to try using one of the relaxation techniques discussed earlier in this chapter. Also, try to limit the use of your bed to sleeping. Avoid watching television, doing paperwork, eating, or reading in your bed. Do these things in another room. In this way you will associate your bed only with sleeping, which may decrease the amount of time it takes for you to fall asleep when you go to bed. Remember, if you sleep enough, you will feel rested, view things in a more positive light, and be a more effective problem solver.

Eat a Well-Balanced Diet

You have probably heard the expression "You are what you eat." You can argue the merits of this saying, but there is no denying that your diet influences your body's ability to function optimally. A balanced diet provides your body with the nutrition required to have the energy and health necessary to function well. A poor diet can result not only in a lack of energy but also an inability for your body to fight off illness.

One of the major problems with stress and diet is that many people tend to eat less nutritious foods when they are under stress. Eating more junk food when under stress can establish a vicious circle. The more stressed you become, the poorer your eating habits; the poorer your eating habits, the less able your body is to help you deal with stress. So make an extra effort to eat balanced and nutritious meals, especially when you are under stress.

Exercise

Just as nutrition is important to your general well-being, so is physical fitness. The more physically fit you are, the greater your ability to handle the physical demands of stress. Unfortunately, when we are under stress, most of us are less, rather than more, physically active. The less physically active you are, the less physically fit you become, so the physical effects of stress will be greater.

Many people who regularly exercise or work out claim that it helps them manage stress. There is also growing scientific evidence that exercise provides benefits beyond general physical fitness. For example, endorphins (the body's "feel good" hormones) are released after a certain level of physical activity is reached. You should establish a regular exercise routine and stick to it, especially when your stress level increases.

Develop Support Systems

Don't try to do it alone! Life can be very difficult and stressful at times, and you need to be able to turn to others for support. This may mean having relationships with people you can talk to when life is stressful. Or it may mean building relationships with people who can offer more tangible support, like looking after your child occasionally so you can have a break. Remember the saying we mentioned in Chapter 12, "It takes a whole village to raise a child." Don't be afraid to reach out to others. Of course, an effective support system needs to go in both directions. Make sure you reciprocate by supporting those who help you, or your support system will collapse.

Maintain a Sense of Humor

When people are under stress, they tend to lose their sense of humor. They may fail to see any of the humor in what is going on in their life. This is unfortunate because humor can be a very effective way to manage stress. Laughing about things and about ourselves can really help us maintain a more realistic perspective about what is happening to us. Laughing also makes us feel good, and it can break tension. So try not to take yourself too seriously, and look for the humor in the situation. Sometimes laughter really can be the best medicine!

You need a big dose of humor when you have a strong-willed child. Such a child truly can test your patience. However, if you understand the role of your thoughts and change them when necessary, you are less likely to lose your patience. When you do lose your patience, minimize the negative effects by using the four Rs: recognize, remove yourself, review, and respond. Finally, by evaluating and minimizing the stress in your life, you will increase your patience and make life more fun. The nine ways we recommend you manage stress are summarized in Table 14-1. Developing patience with a strong-willed child is not easy, but it can be done!

Managing the Stress in Your Life	*TABLE 14-1*

- Identify and reduce stressors.
- Take a break or change gears.
- Learn how to relax.
- Learn effective problem-solving strategies.

- Get enough rest.
- Eat a well-balanced diet.
- Exercise.
- Develop support systems.
- Maintain a sense of humor.

15

Building Positive Self-Esteem

Jim and Jon are five-year-old twins who live with their parents and infant sister. Their kindergarten teacher describes both boys as very popular students who are academically ahead of most of their classmates. Their teacher also believes they have above-average artistic and musical talent. The boys are average in terms of weight and height. Both boys are involved in a number of sports even though their athletic abilities are below average. The boys have a good relationship with their parents and sister. Their teacher and parents consider the boys attractive, popular, and gifted.

How do you think Jim and Jon would rate on self-esteem? Well, it may surprise you to know that Jim was found to have very high self-esteem, while Jon's self-esteem was well below average. How can this happen?

How Does Self-Esteem Develop?

A child's self-esteem starts to develop at a very young age and continues to develop throughout the rest of his life. Therefore, as a parent, you have daily opportunities to help your child develop positive self-esteem.

Before looking at the major factors that influence the development of positive self-esteem, let's examine self-esteem a little more closely. Self-esteem is tied closely to self-confidence. Children, like adults, actually may have positive self-esteem in some areas of their life but not in others. For example, a child may have positive self-esteem about his popularity and social skills and negative self-esteem about his academic skills.

Although self-esteem can be broken down into different areas, when we refer to a child's self-esteem, we generally mean the child's overall, or global, self-esteem. In other words, how does he feel generally about himself as a person? Global self-esteem depends on his accomplishments in each area and his belief about what areas are most important. A child's global self-esteem may be negative even if he views himself positively in most areas. In the example at the beginning of this chapter, the difference between Jon and Jim's self-esteem came from the level of importance each boy placed on different areas of functioning. Jon viewed physical and athletic ability as the most important personal quality and wanted to be known as a good athlete. Although he excelled in all other areas, his global self-esteem was negative because of his poor performance in the one area he valued the most. His brother, Jim, viewed popularity and academics as the most important personal qualities and physical and athletic ability as secondary. As a result, Jim's overall self-esteem was very positive.

As is clear from the example of Jim and Jon, the two major factors that contribute to a child's quality of self-esteem are his accomplishments or level of skill in various areas (such as social interactions, school performance, or sports) and his relative evaluation of his competence in the areas *he* deems most important. Therefore, as a parent, you should strive to help your child develop the skills necessary to achieve to the best of his ability, focus on his strengths and minimize his weaknesses, and help him feel good about his strengths.

Why Is Positive Self-Esteem Important?

It is important to help your child build positive self-esteem. Children's self-esteem is related to numerous positive outcomes in life, including success in school, positive interpersonal relationships, and the ability to resist peer pressure. Children with positive self-esteem tend to be more successful in almost all areas of life than children with self-esteem that is negative.

Some people believe that positive self-esteem does not lead to things such as success in school but rather that success in school leads to higher self-esteem. In part, this is true. The relationship between self-esteem and success in life goes in both directions. So it is important for you to focus both on helping your child succeed by teaching him the skills necessary for success and on helping him view his level of ability in a positive way.

Ways to Build Positive Self-Esteem

Developing positive self-esteem in strong-willed children is especially important. Many strong-willed children receive frequent negative feedback and relatively little positive feedback from others. Over time, this situation can start eroding a child's self-esteem. Therefore, it is important that you, as a parent, make an extra effort to build your child's positive self-esteem. Let's look at how you can do this.

Encourage Your Child's Interests and Abilities

We all have strengths and weaknesses, as well as different things in which we are interested. Children are no exception! While you should try to expose your child to many things and activities from an early age, as his parent you also need to develop an awareness of what things he is most interested in and of his strengths and weaknesses in these and other areas. As he grows older, continue to provide exposure to a variety of things but strongly encourage the development of skills in areas where he shows strong aptitude or ability. For some children, this may be a certain sport, while for others, it may be a special hobby or a skill such as art.

It is important to try to further develop the skills and interests in which your child shows particular promise. This will help him feel he is better than, or at least as good as, other children his age in at least one activity. This does not mean you should focus your child's activities in only one area—he should be exposed to many different activities and areas. However, as your child grows older, his interests and special abilities will become more apparent. As this happens, encourage him to focus his time and effort in those areas.

Be careful to help him pursue his interests, as opposed to your interests.

Offer Frequent Encouragement and Praise

All parents want their children to feel good about themselves. One way you can achieve this is by frequently encouraging and praising your child's efforts. If you think you already praise and encourage your child frequently, consider that in our experience most parents think they praise and encourage their children much more than they actually do. They often think about their child in a positive sense without always communicating those thoughts very well.

Try to make a conscious effort every day to increase the number of times you encourage and praise your child. The sidebar "Ways to Praise and Encourage Your Child" later in this chapter suggests things you can say. Try not to use just one or two phrases repeatedly. Using many different expressions of encouragement and praise will be more effective. Also, do not focus exclusively on verbal praise. Offer a lot of physical expressions of praise such as high fives, pats on the back, ruffling of hair, and hugs. Such nonverbal expressions can be especially powerful. Apply the principles you learned during Week 2 of the five-week program, when you practiced praising your strong-willed child. (See Chapter 7.)

Recognize Your Child's Normal Accomplishments

We all like to have our accomplishments recognized. Make sure you recognize your child's normal and everyday accomplishments instead of waiting until he does something outstanding. In addition to praise, think of other ways to further recognize his accomplishments. For example, display his artwork or other work from preschool or school on the refrigerator door. You might even consider having some of his best artwork framed and hung in your home. (This makes a great conversation piece when you have guests!) Place other things he makes or builds in some prominent place in the house. If possible, take one of your child's masterpieces to your workplace so it will be on display if he visits you. Also, make a big deal about sending your child's work to other people such as grandparents or other relatives. Have your child make things to be included in special-occasion gifts for family members and close friends.

By recognizing your child's normal accomplishments, you help him become aware of his own abilities and encourage him to continue his efforts. This sense of accomplishment is strengthened by displaying his work and having others also recognize his accomplishments. Be sure to attend not only to the final product but also to the effort that goes into your child's accomplishments.

Encourage Your Child to Make Decisions

One of our goals as parents is to help our children develop self-discipline. By encouraging him in making decisions from an early age, you can help your child develop not only self-discipline but also positive self-esteem. By making decisions, your child will develop a sense of self-control and accomplishment. As he makes "good" decisions, over time he will

Ways to Praise and Encourage Your Child

"That's great!"
"You're doing such a great job!"
"That's the way!"
"You should be very proud of yourself!"
"That's the way to do it!"
"Wow!"
"Good for you!"
"You're getting better every day!"
"You can do it!"
"That's it!"
"You've just about got it!"
"You've figured it out!"
"You're so good at that!"
"Way to go!"
"You make it look easy!"
"You're the best!"
"Good work!"

develop both a sense of ability and self-worth. If you as a parent make all the decisions for your young child, he will have more difficulty making decisions when he is older. The message he may hear is that he is not capable of making decisions or that you do not have confidence in his ability to make decisions. Furthermore, he will never have a chance to experience the feeling of success for good decisions and of failure for poor decisions.

We are not recommending that young children be made responsible for major decisions or the majority of the decisions in their life. However, children should be given the responsibility for making some decisions from a very early age. For example, during the early years, you can let your child choose which of two shirts he would like to wear. Limit the number of options from which he may choose, saying something like, "Would you like this or this?" Too many options can overwhelm a young child and frustrate you—especially when you have to wait an eternity for a decision! When he consistently does well selecting from two options, gradually give him more options from which to choose when making decisions. As your child grows older, allow him to make increasingly more decisions in a wider variety of areas of his life. In sum, children should learn how to make decisions from an early age, and as they grow older, their decision making should expand.

Let Your Child Take Some Risks

Parents naturally want to protect their children from failure. However, you do your child a disservice if you always protect him to the point of not allowing him to take risks that may lead to failure. Of course, we are not talking about taking risks that involve dangerous activities. Also, you should not let your child take a lot of risks. At the same time, do not be afraid to let your child experience some failure. By taking some risks, your child will learn that he can do things he did not think he could. Successfully taking risks builds positive self-esteem. The key is for you to try to make sure most of the risks will end on a positive note.

Let's look at an example. Many parents would not let their three-year-old carry a breakable plate from the dinner table to the kitchen sink. However, if you think there is a good chance that your three-year-old can take the plate to the sink without dropping it, let him try. If he succeeds, praise him and let him know how much you appreciate his helping around the house. In this situation, your child would experience success in something he had not done before and also would experience praise from you. As a result, he will feel more confident in his abilities and pleased with his contribution to helping around the house.

What would happen if he dropped the plate? Well, you would have known there was a risk of that happening and prepared yourself not to become upset. View the plate's breaking as an accident and handle it matter-of-factly. This failure, like any other single event, is unlikely to have a major impact on self-esteem; only repeated failure damages self-esteem. That is why you want your child to succeed most of the time. However, learning how to handle failure is also important. If you never allow him to experience failure, he most likely will have a very difficult time later in life when you can no longer protect him from failure. Thus, try to view your child's failure as a chance to teach him how to cope with it. To make failure a learning experience, handle his failure matter-of-factly and praise him for his effort rather than the outcome. Soon after the failure, have him try a task at which he will probably succeed. Finally, let your child know that failure happens for a variety of reasons, not because he is a bad person.

In summary, the confidence from taking risks and succeeding in new tasks can really boost a child's self-esteem. At the same time, a little bit of failure early in life is not a bad thing, especially if parents help the child view minor failures as a chance to learn how to cope with failure.

Give Your Child Responsibilities

As we discussed in Chapter 12, children need to grow up believing that they make an important and meaningful contribution to their family. One way of achieving this is to give your child household responsibilities from an early age. In many families, this might involve giving him specific chores that contribute to the family and home. For a young child, the initial goal is not to have him do some job to perfection but to help him develop a sense of accomplishment and contribution to the family. See the box "Some Suggested Chores for a Young Child" for ideas.

You might have your young child dust the furniture in your living room. The goal is for him to feel good about helping, not do a perfect job of dusting. At first you will probably need to offer a lot of encouragement and praise to help him to feel good about dusting and helping the family. Over time he should develop more willingness to do the job out of a sense of contributing to the family.

In many families, parents wait until their child is older before introducing chores. Then they become upset because the child does not feel a sense of responsibility to participate

Some Suggested Chores for a Young Child

- Help set the dinner table. For a very young child this might initially involve just placing a napkin on the table for each person.
- Put away toys.
- Help water plants.
- Help dust.
- Help vacuum. This could involve helping push the vacuum cleaner or picking up objects on the carpet, such as shoes, so that the parent can vacuum the carpet under the objects.
- Place his dirty clothes in a certain location, such as a laundry basket or hamper.

in household chores. A sense of responsibility and desire to contribute to the family need to be cultivated from a very early age.

Remember, with young children it is important not to pay too much attention to the end result. Initially, you may need to go back and redo your child's job. When this is necessary, do not let your child see you redo the job. If he does, the message he receives might well be that he cannot do the job to your satisfaction. This would decrease, not increase, his self-esteem. Remember, the initial focus for a young child is to help him develop a sense of wanting to help. As he grows older, you can focus more on how to do the job properly.

Don't Demand Perfection

Some parents believe that when their child is not perfect, it reflects poorly on them as parents. If you tend to think this way, it is extremely important for you to come to grips with the fact that there is no perfect child, just as there is no perfect adult or perfect parent. All of us have our strengths and weaknesses. If you expect perfection of yourself, you are setting yourself up for failure. Likewise, if you expect your child to be perfect, you are going to be disappointed, and your child will learn that he can never quite measure up to your expectations. As a result, he will develop a sense of not being good enough to please you. Since most children want to please their parents, such a situation likely will lead him to develop low self-esteem. Also, putting too much pressure on your child to be perfect may backfire and result in his becoming resentful and rebellious.

Do not demand perfection. Instead, encourage your child's best effort. Remember that your child needs to know you accept him unconditionally.

Avoid Using Absolutes When Describing Your Child

Try to resist the temptation to talk about your child in absolute terms, especially when the terms have negative connotations. Avoid saying your child *always* does something wrong or *never* does something right. For example, do not say, "You are always so messy!" or "You never have any respect for me." Parents usually make such absolute statements when they are upset about something their child has done. If you use absolute terms when talking to or about your child, he may start viewing himself as "messy," "disrespectful," or whatever label you have applied to him. If he believes you see him as always being a certain way, he may lose motivation to change.

Instead of using absolutes, focus on your child's behavior within a particular situation. Describe what you observe in that situation. Rather than saying, "You are always so messy," you could say, "You have really messed up your room this afternoon." This does not label your child as messy.

Limit Negative Feedback

No one, child or adult, likes to be criticized. However, many parents make more negative statements than positive statements to their young children. This is especially true for parents with a strong-willed child. You may find yourself repeatedly saying things like "No," "Don't do that," and "Stop that."

In some situations, parents may start off providing positive feedback, but the final result is negative. A good example is a backhanded compliment, in which a parent starts by giving positive feedback but then turns it into negative feedback. A parent might say, "Jake, you did such a good job picking up your toys—why don't you do that all the time? Most of the time I have to remind you over and over to pick up your toys. If you would just pick them up right away, I wouldn't have to get mad and yell at you so much." This type of feedback will unfortunately be remembered as criticism and nagging. Backhanded compliments will have the opposite effect of what you desire.

Try to be mostly positive in the feedback you give to your child. For every instance of negative feedback you give him, try to give positive feedback three or four times. This will be a challenge, but it can enhance your child's self-esteem and help you see the positive aspects of his strong-willed behavior. Try to comment on your child's appropriate expressions of his determination, independence, assertiveness, and confidence.

One other type of negative feedback is overusing the word *no*. Many parents fall into a habit of saying "no" to their child's many minor requests. At times they sound like a continually occurring "no" recording. There is a saying we like that addresses the problem of routinely saying "no" to our children: Say "yes" when you can and "no" when you must.

Don't Make Promises You Might Not Keep

When you repeatedly make and break promises to your child, he may believe that you do not care about or respect him enough to follow through with your promises. If this happens, he may start questioning his own self-worth. When a child starts questioning his worthiness, his self-esteem will suffer.

Keeping promises is also important for another reason— you want your child to view you as honest and true to your word. If you, as a parent, are honest and true to your word, your child will likely develop these traits. In the long run, such traits will help maintain his self-esteem.

The surest way to keep your promises is to think about what you are promising. Before you speak, ask yourself, "Will

I be sure to follow through on this?" If you are not sure you will, do not make a promise.

Teach and Encourage Your Child to Use Positive Self-Talk

Try to encourage your child to say positive things about himself. When he does something good, teach him to say something positive such as, "I did a great job!" How do you teach your child to use such positive self-talk? As we explained in Chapter 2, one of the most effective teaching methods is modeling. To model positive self-talk, look for times during the day when you can compliment yourself out loud. These situations do not have to be the occasional times when you really excel but can be whenever you do routine tasks well. For example, you might say, "I think this sandwich that I just made is great!" Then, when you hear your child say something positive about himself, make sure you acknowledge it and express agreement with him. The more positive things your child says about himself, the more he will believe them and internalize the positive feelings about himself.

You also can encourage your child to use more positive self-talk by the way you provide positive feedback to him. For example, rather than saying, "I'm so proud of you for . . . ," you can rephrase the feedback to "You should be so proud of yourself for . . ." Such phrasing of positive feedback can help him internalize positive feelings about himself. Combine this type of feedback with feedback that expresses your feelings about your child. Ideally, you should provide a mixture of feedback that conveys the message of how you feel and how your child should feel about his accomplishments and behavior.

Spend Quality Time with Your Child

Spending time with your child gives him the message that you care for and enjoy being with him. It is impossible to say just how much time a parent should ideally spend with her child. Different families have different constraints on time. However, you should try to spend as much time with your young child as possible within those constraints.

Even more significant than the amount of time is the quality of the time you spend with your child. Spending hours watching television with your child is not high-quality time. Quality time involves having fun with your child and giving him your undivided attention. As we discussed in Chapter 12, having fun with your child is very important because it communicates that you like and value him. Such positive messages will enhance his self-esteem.

Be Accepting of Your Child

A major component of being in a loving and caring relationship is knowing that you are accepted in spite of all your flaws. Children need to feel that their parents love them regardless of their behavior. Continually communicate love and affection for your child. Let your child know you love him even though you might not like the way he behaves at times. This separation of a child's personal worth and his behavior is especially important for strong-willed children, as their behavior is often a source of difficulty.

In summary, we have presented a number of ways you can increase your strong-willed child's self-esteem:

- Encourage your child's interests and abilities.
- Offer frequent encouragement and praise to your child.
- Recognize your child's accomplishments.
- Encourage your child to make decisions.
- Let your child take some risks.
- Give your child responsibilities.
- Don't demand that your child be perfect.
- Avoid using absolutes when describing your child.
- Limit negative feedback to your child.
- Don't make promises to your child you might not keep.

- Teach and encourage your child to use positive self-talk.
- Spend quality time with your child.
- Be accepting of your child.

These techniques are important because your child's self-esteem is tied to his behavior and the reactions he receives to his behavior. Therefore, in addition to the strategies presented in this chapter, the parenting techniques that you learned in Part II for improving your child's behavior also will enhance his self-esteem.

16

Teaching Your Child Basic Social Skills

It probably comes as no surprise to you that many strong-willed children have problems interacting with other children (and adults). The skills you learned throughout our five-week program will help you manage and improve your child's behavior in general. In this brief chapter, we will focus on a method you can use to teach your child several basic social skills (e.g., appropriately getting someone's attention, waiting your turn, and sharing) that can improve his relationships with others. The method we present in this chapter is intended for use with children who are at least five years old. It is at this age that children start being able to think more effectively about how to manage their own behavior.

We will first discuss the basic method for teaching social skills and then provide examples of how you can use it to teach selected skills. It should be noted that the basic skill of *listening* is being taught and modeled throughout the process of teaching all social skills. Do not move ahead with teaching social skills until your child has learned the basic listening steps (i.e., eyes on me; mouth closed; ears open). Listening is a foundational skill for learning other social skills and should be modeled consistently by parents. Don't forget to listen to your child when it is his turn to talk!

There are five basic steps to teaching your child social skills:

1. Explain the skill.
2. Model (demonstrate) the skill.
3. Have your child role-play the skill.
4. Provide feedback to your child.
5. Encourage your child to practice the skill.

Explain the Skill

First make eye contact with your child and give him your full attention. Allow time for your child to focus on you and what you are about to say. Then, briefly define and explain the skill you will be teaching your child. Remember to be clear and specific and use very few words in describing the skill. Again, just give a brief description of the skill, not a lengthy lesson on why the skill is important.

Model the Skill

Young children learn social skills best through observing others. It is a fact that they imitate the behaviors of those around them (good or bad). Modeling is an opportunity for your child to see you use the skill. Demonstrate the skill by showing him how to do it. Teach your child all the steps involved in the skill (talk out loud about what you are doing/thinking). Be sure to give more than one example of a situation in which you model the skill. Make sure the situations you use make sense to your child. Don't be too serious—make these teachable moments fun and entertaining.

Have Your Child Role-Play the Skill

Your child needs to practice the skill before using it in real life. This gives you the chance to provide feedback and help him improve his skill level. During the role play, your child will practice the skill while you pretend to be another child (or

adult). You can make it into a mini-play with your child helping to set the stage (let him decide where the "play" is going
to happen, what props you both need, how you should play
your part, etc.). In other words, get your child involved in the
process. Remember, you are not simply telling your child what
to do. Your child is practicing how to behave in social situations. He is also showing you that he knows what to do. One
of the most important factors in successful role playing is
making it fun. If you make it too serious, he will not want to
participate.

Provide Feedback to Your Child

Immediately after the role play, provide your child with positive feedback on what he did well. As you learned in Chapter 7, it is important to be very specific in your praise (tell him
exactly what he did well). For example, you might say, "Great!
You looked right at me when I was talking," or "Wow, you
were very quiet." If he needs improvement, provide brief and
very specific suggestions on what he can do to make his use
of the skill even better. Be positive and encouraging. Have him
role-play the skill again ("Let's try it again!") and focus on his
improvement ("I knew you could do it"). Remember, it is your
feedback and positive reinforcement that will change your
child's behavior. It is very important to be patient and reinforce every step along the way.

Encourage Your Child to Practice the Skill

Encourage your child to practice the skill when he is with
other children. Try to have him start practicing the skill in situations where you think he can succeed (e.g., when he is with
children with whom he typically plays well). After he has had
a chance to practice, ask him if he has tried to use the skill.
If he has used the skill, ask him how it went. Be encouraging
about any positive feedback he provides. If it did not go well,
discuss what he could try differently. You can then use modeling and role playing again to help address specific issues. If

your child seems discouraged, you might say, "I know this is hard, but you can do it." These words offer support and allow you to remain positive and encouraging.

Now let's provide some examples about how to apply this five-step method to teach children basic social skills. We are going to provide three examples: getting someone's attention to ask a question, waiting your turn, and sharing. Of course, the same method can be used to teach your child a wide variety of social skills to help improve his social interactions with both peers and adults.

Example 1: Getting Someone's Attention

The ability to get someone's attention in order to ask a question or join into a conversation is an important one for young children. Many strong-willed children have a hard time getting someone's attention in an appropriate manner. They often interrupt or make demands to be heard. Teaching your child to appropriately get someone's attention is a valuable social skill. So, let's see how a parent might use the five-step method to teach her child this skill.

> *Mother: Have you ever wanted to ask someone a question while they are busy talking to someone else?*
>
> *Child: (Nods yes).*
>
> *Mother: Well, then let's play a game to learn a good way to get someone's attention so you can ask them a question. First, when someone is busy talking, you should only interrupt when you have an important question to ask. (Mother briefly pauses and gives her child time to think about what she just said). Then, you should wait until they stop talking for a moment. Then, you say, "Excuse me." Now, are you ready to play a game to learn exactly how to do it?*
>
> *Child: How do we play the game?*

> Mother: We are going to pretend we are at your
>   school. First, you pretend that you are Ms. Wood,
>   your teacher. Pretend she is talking to another
>   teacher during recess. I'll pretend to be you, and
>   you want to ask Ms. Wood a question. Are you
>   ready to start?
> Child: Yes!
> Mother: OK, you start pretending to be Ms. Wood
>   talking to another teacher. (Encourage child to
>   talk out loud as if talking to another teacher. If
>   he has a hard time with this, suggest things he
>   might say.)
> Mother: (Pretends to talk like her son.) I really want
>   to ask Ms. Wood if I can go to the bathroom, but
>   she's busy talking to Ms. Davis. (Mother starts
>   walking toward her child.) I need to go stand
>   next to her and wait for her to look at me. When
>   she stops talking, I can say, "Excuse me," and
>   then ask if I can go to the bathroom. (Mother
>   then stands next to her child and waits until he
>   stops his pretend talking and looks at her.)
>   Excuse me, Ms. Wood. May I go to the bathroom?
> Child: Yes, you can go.
> Mother: How did I do?
> Child: Good!
> Mother: Now let's switch. It's your turn to be you, and
>   I'll pretend to be your teacher.

The child then role-plays the same situation. The mother provides positive feedback and encouragement to her child. Remember to keep any negative feedback brief and specific. After your child is successful with that role-playing situation, come up with a different situation (focused on the same social skill) to model and role-play. For example, you might work on how to best interrupt another child to ask if you can play with one of his toys. Remember, a child's attention span is short. It is our recommendation that you spend no more than five minutes at a time working on these role plays. Repetition and fun are the keys to teaching these skills.

Example 2: Waiting Your Turn

Discuss with your child how hard it is to wait your turn. Explain that it is important to wait quietly (and not get mad or bother others). Discuss what he can do while waiting (e.g., think about all the letters of the alphabet he knows, watch what others around him are doing, think about something fun). Be encouraging and tell him you know that he can learn to wait his turn. A possible situation to model and role-play might include waiting in line to use the slide on the school playground.

Here is a sample of what might be said as a parent and child go through some of the steps:

> *Mother: How many children can go down the slide at one time?*
> *Child: Only one.*
> *Mother: Is that the rule?*
> *Child: Yes, my teacher said so.*
> *Mother: It's hard to wait in line, isn't it?*
> *Child: Yes!*
> *Mother: Let's play the pretend game to practice waiting for your turn. I'll pretend to be you waiting in line for the slide. You pretend to be your friend Joey, who is also standing in line.*
> *Child: OK.*
> *Mother: (Mother pretends to be her son and talks in a voice like his.) I'm going to take some deep breaths and slowly count to five. 1 . . . 2 . . . 3 . . . 4 . . . 5. Then, I'm going to tell myself that, "I can wait for my turn." How did I do?*
> *Child: You did a good job, Mom. But I can count to 10!*
> *Mother: I know you can! So now you play yourself waiting in line—and you can count as high as you want!*
> *Child: OK. (The child then role-plays the skill. Mother stands in the pretend line, as Joey, and starts yelling.)*

> *Mother: (Mother provides feedback.) You did such a good job of waiting in line! You ignored Joey. You waited for your turn while you quietly counted. I bet the next time you are excited and have to wait in line at school you'll be able to do the same thing to help you wait quietly.*

Note that the skill is explained, modeled by the mother, practiced by the child in a role play, positive feedback is given, and the child is encouraged to practice the skill at school. This is the five-step method!

Example 3: Sharing

Don't expect children under the age of five to share well. From a developmental perspective, it's hard for young children to willingly share. Sharing can be most effectively taught as a social skill when children are at least five years old. Start by explaining different ways of sharing (such as taking turns with crayons or markers at school). Stress the importance of using "nice talk" when asking someone to share. Situations to model and role-play might include having to share craft supplies at school. Here is a brief sample of what might be said while teaching the skill of sharing.

> *Mother: Let's pretend we are working on an art project at school. I'll pretend to be you. You pretend to be Nathan.*
> *Child: I like Nathan.*
> *Mother: I know you do. (Then, she pretends to be her child and talks in a happy voice.) Will you please share your crayons with me?*
> *Child: I'm using the blue one.*
> *Mother: OK. May I use it when you are finished?*
> *Child: Yes. Here it is!*
> *Mother: Thanks. Do you want to use the red one that I was using?*
> *Child: Sure.*

This is a straightforward role play that shows the child the steps to sharing. By helping your child learn how to share well, you can have a significant impact on his ability to interact well with other children.

In conclusion, the three examples we provided are clearly important social skills that young children need to learn. However, there are many other social skills (e.g., asking someone to play, accepting "no") that you can teach your child using this five-step method. This method provides a framework for teaching children how to behave in a wide variety of social situations. Remember, the five-step method is recommended for use with children who are at least five years old. Some children catch on right away, and others take months to learn a skill. Be patient and remember that if you follow the steps for teaching the skill, your child will eventually learn. Most important, when he sees you regularly using good social skills during your everyday life, you are teaching by example. Your commitment to teaching social skills is an investment in the future. Over his lifetime, good social skills will greatly benefit your child.

PART IV

Solving Some Common Behavior Problems: Additional Recommendations

At this point you should better understand your child's behavior (Part I), know the basic skills to address your child's general behavior problems (Part II), and understand how to create a solid foundation for behavioral change (Part III). In this final part, we discuss how to use what you've learned in this book thus far, as well as some additional strategies, to handle specific behavior problem areas for two- to six-year-old children.

17

Specific Problem Behaviors

Among common problem behaviors of two- to six-year-old children are temper tantrums, aggressive behavior, mealtime behavior problems, dressing problems, problems in the car, bedtime and sleep problems, lying, and sibling rivalry. We selected these specific behavior problem areas to focus on in Part IV because our surveys of parents indicated that they are of significant concern to many parents, especially parents of strong-willed children.

Before you begin reading our suggestions for dealing with these specific behavior problems, it is very important that you understand that the strategies we present in Part IV should be used only in combination with the skills and strategies you have learned in the earlier parts of the book. It is the combined use of all of these skills that will prove to be most effective in helping change the negative aspects of your strong-willed child's behavior.

Temper Tantrums

Temper tantrums are very common, especially for young strong-willed children. Tantrums can range from whining and crying to biting, kicking, throwing objects, and falling to the ground. When a tantrum occurs, it usually has a specific purpose. That is, temper tantrums are usually an attempt to gain attention, to get something, or to avoid something. No matter what the reason for the temper tantrum, you should communicate to your child that it is unacceptable.

If your child is prone to having frequent temper tantrums, remember that you will not be able to eliminate them altogether. All children have temper tantrums at some point. Your goal should be to decrease their frequency and their intensity. The following recommendations can help:

- **Attend to and praise your child's appropriate behavior.** This will reduce the probability of tantrums occurring. Especially use your attending and praising skills (from Part II) in situations that are frustrating to your child. Whenever he uses appropriate ways of dealing with frustration rather than having a tantrum, be sure to acknowledge it with praise and attention.
- **Temper tantrums tend to occur more often when a child is hungry or tired.** Try to make sure that your child has enough sleep and eats regularly.
- **Look for a pattern in the timing of his temper tantrums.** For example, do they occur mostly in the evening when your child is tired or before meals when he might be hungry? If you identify a pattern, you should try to rearrange his schedule to decrease the likelihood of tantrums.
- **Intervene early, either before the temper tantrum starts or as soon as possible after it starts.** Most children do not go from behaving appropriately to having a temper tantrum in a matter of seconds. More often, they first engage in inappropriate behavior such as talking back, crying, or yelling. In most cases, you probably know when a tantrum is about to occur. Whenever you have the gut feeling that it is about to happen, intervene at that point—don't wait. For example, use time-out when your child starts talking back to you—don't wait until his negative behavior escalates before you react.
- **Ignore temper tantrums.** This is not easy, but it ensures that your child does not receive attention for his inappropriate behavior. Ignoring does not include leaving your

child alone when this is potentially dangerous. Keep him in eyesight. Follow the guidelines for ignoring in Chapter 8.

- **When a temper tantrum occurs, make sure it does not work!** Do not let your child avoid any responsibilities by having a temper tantrum. If your child has the temper tantrum because you said "no," do not change your mind.

- **Try to relax and remain as calm as possible during your child's temper tantrum.** Act as if you're in control and deal with the situation as matter-of-factly as possible. *Never* yell back or give in to the temper tantrum.

- **Acknowledge the fact that your child is upset—but only after he has settled down (and the tantrum is over).** For example, you could state, "I'm sorry that you were so angry, but having a temper tantrum is not OK." If your child is older than four, at a later time you also can ask him what would have been a better way for him to handle the situation that led to the temper tantrum.

- **After your child's temper tantrum is over, move on.** Put the episode behind you.

- **Help your child learn to express himself with words.** As children develop better language skills and the ability to express their feelings and desires, temper tantrums typically decrease.

Aggressive Behavior

Many young strong-willed children hit, push, bite, throw things, or destroy objects as a means of getting their way or something they want. These types of aggression are most common in children two to three years old. As children grow older, physical aggression tends to decline. Unfortunately, verbal aggression often increases. Fortunately, there are some things parents can do to limit aggressive behavior:

- **Attend to and praise your child when he uses behaviors other than aggression to deal with frustration and difficult situations.** For example, praise him when you see him walk away from a child who was provoking him.

- **After the crisis has passed, try to teach your child alternatives to aggression.** For a two- to four-year-old child, you can offer him some alternatives. For instance, you can say, "When you feel angry, take a deep breath and come talk to me." For a child over four, encourage him to think of some ways of handling the situation other than by aggression. If he has difficulty coming up with ideas, you can suggest some appropriate ideas (e.g., helping him find appropriate words to express how he feels).
- **Limit your child's screen time.** As we discussed in Chapter 3, there is a high incidence of aggression on television and other forms of media.
- **Limit your child's exposure to real acts of aggression.** Try to prevent your child from being around aggressive children and adults. If you are around aggressive adults, walk away from them rather than respond to their aggression. By doing so, you are modeling appropriate behavior for your child.
- **Make sure your child's aggressive behavior does not result in him getting his way or being able to get something he desires.** If he grabs or takes something from another child, he (or you) should return that object to the other child immediately.
- **Try to remain calm and handle the aggressive episode as matter-of-factly as possible.** Remember you need to be a good role model. If you lose your temper you are not teaching him appropriate behavior.
- **Use immediate time-out for aggressive behavior.** Do not give a warning for aggressive behavior. Giving a child a warning for aggressive behavior is like telling him that he always has one free punch before any discipline will occur.
- **Acknowledge your child's feelings, but make sure he understands that aggression is not acceptable.** For example, after you have dealt with the aggressive behavior, you can say, "I know you were angry, but you must not hit someone else—no matter how angry you are."

Mealtime Behavior Problems

Some young children are frequently up and down at the dinner table, throw food, grab food from the table, eat with their mouths open, or talk with their mouths full. Any one of these behaviors can be very frustrating to parents, especially when they occur continually. When such mealtime behaviors occur constantly, parents often will respond by nagging and threatening their child. Such patterns lead to mealtimes that are unpleasant for both parents and child!

The most important step you can take toward improving your child's mealtime behavior is to make mealtimes more positive. In Chapter 12 we discussed the importance of family mealtimes and made several suggestions for making mealtimes more positive. Please review those recommendations if you are having problems with your child's behavior at mealtimes. In addition to those recommendations, here are some others that can help you manage mealtime behavior problems:

- **You and other family members should model good mealtime behaviors.** Sometimes parents or older siblings chew with their mouths open or frequently leave the dinner table. It is hard to expect children to follow mealtime rules when their parents and older siblings do not follow them.
- **If your child misbehaves during mealtime, there should be an immediate consequence.** For example, if he throws food, he should be placed in time-out. An easy way of implementing time-out at the dinner table is to pull your child's chair, with him sitting in it, away from the table. While he is away from the table, you should carry on a conversation but exclude your child from the conversation.
- **As a general rule, if you use time-out three times with your child during a single meal, then that meal is finished for him.** Remember, no snacks or dessert when meals are not eaten!

Dressing Problems

Many young strong-willed children resist getting dressed. This resistance might take the form of a child actively resisting his parent trying to dress him or the child's insisting on wearing an inappropriate type of clothing. Although we recommend giving children some choice in deciding what to wear, wearing a sweater in ninety-degree weather is not acceptable!

Also be aware of what your child is capable of doing in terms of dressing himself. By the age of two to three, most children show an interest in wanting to help dress themselves. By the age of three, most children can put on only large articles of clothing by themselves. By four years old, they can usually fasten large buttons. By five, they typically can dress themselves except for tying their shoelaces. Also, remember that children can take clothes off before they can learn to put them on!

With these limitations in mind, here are some recommendations to follow for managing dressing problems:

- **If deciding what to wear is a problem in the morning, lay out the clothes your child will wear the night before.** It is usually best to lay out these clothes in a place that is not next to his other clothes. This strategy helps minimize him seeing other clothing in the morning and changing his mind—perhaps repeatedly—about what to wear.
- **Give your child some choice in what he wears—but not too much choice.** As we suggested previously, it is typically best to let preschoolers choose between two articles of clothing. For example, ask, "Would you like to wear this red shirt or this blue one?"
- **Allow plenty of time for your child to dress.** In many households, mornings are frantic, with adults and children all dressing under time pressures. However, as you probably well know, it is very difficult to rush a young strong-willed child to get dressed. In many families, the more you try to rush him, the more resistance he offers. Allowing enough time eliminates the "rush factor."

- **Make dressing fun.** Sing songs to your young child. Play music on a stereo. Distract your child by having him look out the window or at a picture on the wall. Have your child name the colors of the clothes you are putting on him.
- **Use frequent attending and praise during dressing.** For example, say, "We are putting this sock over your foot, and we are pulling it up really high. Now we are putting the other sock over your toes, and up over your ankle, and pulling it up really high. Now we are slipping your pants over your feet, and we're pulling them up all the way up to the top."
- **For children who leave home in the morning to go to a child care center, preschool program, or school, it is important to establish a regular morning routine.** For example, when your child awakens, he should brush his teeth, comb his hair, and then dress. He should not be allowed to watch television or play games until after he has dressed and eaten breakfast.
- **If your child tends to stall and not dress in a reasonable amount of time and is at least four years old, you can sometimes make morning routines more fun and effective by playing "beat the clock."** Set a kitchen timer for a reasonable amount of time for him to become fully dressed. If he beats the clock and is dressed before the buzzer goes off, he should be praised and perhaps offered some type of incentive, such as a sticker or the choice of a special breakfast item.

As your child reaches the age of four or five, he should be taking on more responsibility for dressing himself. To help him learn to dress himself, buy clothes that are easy for him to put on. Try to avoid clothes with small buttons or clasps. As your child is learning how to dress himself, make sure you praise him often. Initially, you can teach him to dress himself by taking the first steps in putting an article of clothing on him and then letting him complete the task. For instance, you might start by pulling his socks up to his ankles and then let him pull them up all the way. Or you could put his pants over his feet and have him pull them up. Offer a lot of praise and attending while teaching him to dress himself.

Behavior Problems in the Car

One of the most frustrating situations that parents face is misbehavior in the car. Since the parent is driving, she is limited in what she can do to manage behavior problems.

The primary recommendation for car travel is to *make sure your child is always properly restrained.* Correctly use a car seat, booster seat, or seat belt, depending on your child's size. From a very early age, establish that you do not start the car until everyone in the car, including yourself, is buckled in. Automobile accidents are the leading cause of death for children. The majority of these deaths could be prevented if children were properly restrained. Children who are correctly restrained are not only much safer but also much better behaved while in the car.

The following tactics can also help you prevent problem behavior in the car:

- **Have certain activities that are "car activities."** You might keep a bag of toys for your child to use only while riding in the car.
- **Buy a CD of music that your child likes.** Play it only in the car and only when he is behaving appropriately. As soon as there is any inappropriate behavior, stop the CD until the inappropriate behavior has stopped.
- **For long trips, take snacks and drinks, special games, and picture books or old magazines for your child.** To combat boredom, you also can sing special songs or play "I spy" with objects inside the car, counting games, or alphabet games.
- **Frequently praise and attend in the car when your child is behaving well.** This is the most important tactic. Remember to use your attending and rewarding skills often!

If your child does misbehave in the car, remain calm. Pull the car over to the side of the road and consider your child to be in time-out in his seat. That is, remain in the car, but totally ignore your child until he has settled down and becomes quiet. Remember from Chapter 8 that ignoring means *no* physical contact, *no* verbal contact, and *no* eye contact. After he has been quiet for the length of time that you would normally expect in time-out, acknowledge that he has settled down, start the car up, and continue on your trip. When you're under time pressure, this can be very frustrating. However, your child needs to know that he cannot misbehave in the car. If your child often misbehaves in the car, allow extra time on trips in order to teach him to behave more appropriately.

Stopping the car and imposing a time-out might not work if you are traveling somewhere that your child does not want to go. In this case it is best to continue on your trip. If he is younger than three or four, ignore him to the extent possible. If he is five or older, impose a loss of privilege. You also can use time-out after you have reached your destination; however, time-out is much less effective if it is delayed.

If you have more than one child in the car and they start fighting, stop the car and separate them to the extent possible. Impose time-out for both children as we described several paragraphs earlier. This will not be easy, but it can be effective.

Bedtime and Sleep Problems

Although bedtime and sleep difficulties have many variations, our focus here is on four primary problems: going to bed, difficulty falling asleep, fears and anxieties, and frequent wakenings. These sleep problems are among the most common for young children. In many cases, they are much more of a problem for the parent than they are the child—especially if you are a parent who likes to sleep! When sleep prob-

Average Sleep Patterns of Young Children	TABLE 17-1

Age (in Years)	Average Sleep Pattern
2	11½ hours at night plus a 1½ hour nap
3	11 hours at night plus a 1 hour nap
4–5	12 hours at night (no nap)
6–7	10–11 hours at night (no nap)

lems occur nightly, the family can experience a significant amount of stress.

As you determine whether you have a problem and consider which recommendations apply to you, review the information in Table 17-1, "Average Sleep Patterns of Young Children." This table summarizes the average sleep habits of young children. The times given are averages; individual sleep patterns vary substantially. Some children need less sleep than the average, while others need more than the average.

Problems Going to Bed

Putting a strong-willed child to bed is very frustrating for many parents. Some children refuse to go to bed, while others go to bed but then frequently call out for their parents or come out of their bedroom. All children sometimes resist going to bed or have difficulty falling asleep. This behavior becomes a problem when it occurs frequently.

Bedtime Routines and Rituals. The basic way to prevent problems at bedtime is to make this a consistent and predictable time. Many children with bedtime problems have an inconsistent sleep schedule. It is hard for a child's body to establish a regular sleep/wake cycle unless his bedtime and morning waking time are fairly consistent. If your child goes to bed one night at 8:00 P.M., the next night at 11:00 P.M., and the following night at 9:00 P.M., he will have difficulty developing good sleep habits. Although no one is going to be totally consistent with bedtime, you should at least strive for consistency. Also, if your child is having difficulty sleeping, it is best to awaken him at approximately the same time every day, even on weekends.

Also develop a consistent bedtime ritual. This is a routine that your child goes through every night immediately before going to bed. It should involve about four to seven activities that are quieting and soothing, such as a bath, a snack, brush teeth, a bedtime story, goodnight kisses, and arranging soft animals in his bed. This bedtime ritual should last at least fifteen to twenty minutes. A longer ritual can be difficult to manage every night. If your child is having difficulty settling down at night, make sure the bedtime ritual activities occur in the same sequence every night.

Some parents find that playing "beat the clock" can be helpful in dealing with their child's stalling during the bedtime routine. The parents set a timer for whatever time limit they believe to be reasonable to complete the bedtime routine without rushing. The purpose is not to have the child rush through the routine but rather to prevent stalling. If the child is in bed and has completed all of his routine activities appropriately before the buzzer or alarm goes off, he gets to hear an extra bedtime story. If you use this approach, do not allow your child to have an extra story unless he beats the clock.

Going to bed is a transition for children. Transitions can be difficult for strong-willed children. Therefore, tell your child five to ten minutes beforehand that it will be bedtime in a few minutes. Try to make the transition to bed as smooth as possible. One way to do this is to plan for games and activities to end before bedtime. Once bedtime arrives, do not allow any stalling.

If your child has a habit of requesting a drink or expressing a need to go to the bathroom after the lights have been turned out, try to prepare to avoid these problems. Make sure your child has a drink of water before going to bed, or place a glass of water on his bedside table. Also make sure your child uses the bathroom before going to bed.

Praise and attend to your child during the bedtime routine. Attending to your child during bath, undressing, and other activities during the routine expresses your affection toward your child and acknowledges his efforts.

Make bedtime a loving time with your child. Avoid interruptions. For example, you typically should not answer the telephone during the bedtime routine so the routine can be as consistent and calming as possible. Use this time to show a lot of physical affection toward your child and express your love. As your child grows older, you can talk about the good things that happened during the day and the good things that will happen the next day.

Difficulty Falling Asleep. If your child has a habit of lying in bed for one or two hours after bedtime before he falls asleep, it may help to temporarily move his bedtime to a later time. Move the bedtime to the approximate time he is naturally going to sleep. That way, he probably will fall asleep sooner after going to bed because his body is used to going to sleep at that time. After he is going to sleep consistently at the later bedtime, gradually move the bedtime to an earlier, more appropriate time. However, it is important not to move the bedtime back to the earlier time too quickly. If you're putting your child to bed at 8:00 P.M. but he is not falling asleep until 10:00 P.M., initially move his bedtime to approximately 10:00 P.M. After he is falling asleep quickly and consistently at 10:00 P.M., move his bedtime back to 9:45 P.M. for several nights, then move it back by fifteen minutes every few nights thereafter. Continue this procedure until his bedtime is back to the original time of 8:00 P.M. If you try to move the bedtime back too quickly, your efforts may fail because your child's body is not gradually adjusting to the earlier time of falling asleep.

If your child is still taking a nap, examine when this nap is occurring. If it is late in the afternoon, he may not be tired enough to fall asleep at his regular bedtime. Although we do not recommend eliminating the nap until a child is at least four years old, try to make his nap earlier in the afternoon and perhaps decrease the length of the nap.

If your child gets out of bed and comes out of his bedroom before going to sleep, immediately return him to his room. Do not talk to him or express anger. Rather, pick him up, carry him facing away from you so he cannot cuddle with you, and put him back in his bed. At that point, make eye contact and firmly say, "You need to stay in your bedroom."

Some children do not get out of bed but call out to their parents. See the sidebar "Responding to Your Child's Frequent Calls for You" for a way to handle this bedtime problem.

You cannot make your child fall asleep, but you can control what time he goes to bed and that he stays in his bedroom. The rule should be for your child to stay in his bedroom. Trying to insist that your child stay in his bed and go to sleep can lead to unnecessary conflict. If your child stays in his room but sleeps on the floor near the door, he will soon learn that the bed is the more comfortable place to sleep.

Another response if your child leaves his room before going to sleep is to close the door. If he is used to having his bedroom door open, you can leave it open initially when he goes to bed. Tell him that if he comes out of his bedroom, you will put him back in the bed and close his door. Closing the door in this way is a method of enforcing the rule that your child stay in his room, not an effort to punish or scare him. If you close the door, have a night-light in your child's room so he will not be totally in the dark. Also check on your child regularly (as described later).

Fears and Anxieties. If your child expresses any fear or anxiety about going to bed, such as being afraid of monsters, it is important to address his concern. Remember, young children have very active imaginations and sometimes have difficulty separating fantasy from reality. You can use this to your advantage! Rather than saying there are no such things as monsters, say something such as, "My job as your mom is

Responding to Your Child's Frequent Calls for You

If your child calls out for you, do not respond immediately. Wait at least three minutes before going to check on him. When you go, try not to pick up your child or to lie down next to him in order to help him fall asleep. The problem for many children with sleep difficulties is that they are used to their parents' helping them fall asleep. They learn to rely on their parents, not how to fall asleep easily on their own. Instead, go into his room to reassure him that you are still in the house and to reassure yourself that he is all right. Stay in the room no longer than one minute.

If he calls out again, wait five to seven minutes before going back. Continue this cycle, adding a couple of minutes each time before going in until you are waiting a maximum of ten to fifteen minutes between checks. If you have temporarily moved your child's bedtime later, he will be that much more tired and should be falling asleep after a relatively short period of time.

This procedure can be very difficult for parents. In many cases their child may cry excessively. However, there is no evidence that this harms your child. Unfortunately, you cannot reason with your child about the need to go to sleep. This technique of waiting before going in to check on your child can take up to a week, but if you stick with it, it can be very effective. If you give in and pick your child up or let your child sleep with you, you are reinforcing behavior that you want to stop and the problem can become worse in the future.

to make sure that no monsters come into our house." Another technique that has worked for many families is to buy some spray air freshener and cover the can with paper wrapping on which you've drawn a monster with an *X* through it and written "Monster Repellent." At night before your child goes to bed, you and he can spray the room to assure that no monsters will come into his room during the night. Of course, these techniques will be less effective as your child grows older. If he exhibits significant fear or anxiety about sleeping, you might want to consider seeking professional help.

If your child is concerned about separation from you at bedtime, let him know that you will check on him. You could tell your child, "If you are quiet, I will come check on you in five minutes." Also tell your child that he must stay in the room.

In many cultures, children sleep with their parents during their early childhood. This is not the norm in our culture. However, if you want your child to sleep with you, that is your decision. There is evidence suggesting that while some children naturally make the transition from sleeping in their parents' bed to sleeping in their own bed, many children have difficulty making the transition. We have seen several families in which children in the preteen and early teen years still needed a parent to lie down beside them in order for them to sleep. We believe that if your goal is to have your child sleep on his own, it is most effective to make it a habit early in life.

When your child is easily going to bed and falling asleep rapidly, it is important to praise him in the morning. You might initially want to offer a special item for breakfast or another small treat if he did well the previous night. Do not lecture or nag him if the night did not go well. Focus only on improvements.

Frequent Awakening

Most children wake up several times during the night but fall back to sleep on their own. However, some children have a very difficult time going back to sleep. In most cases, this is because they developed poor sleeping habits at an early age. At least in part this occurs because parents have helped them go back to sleep and they have not learned how to fall asleep on their own. The goal for these children is to help them learn how to fall asleep on their own. Teaching your child to go back to sleep on his own involves a technique similar to the one for helping your child learn to fall asleep at bedtime. Having a consistent bedtime and a bedtime ritual can also reduce problems related to awakening during the night.

If your child is waking up frequently at night, it is important that you put him to bed while he is still awake. Do not help him fall asleep at bedtime. He must learn how to go to sleep on his own.

If your child gets out of bed and comes into your bedroom, follow the same procedure as we described for initially putting him to bed: immediately tell him to go back to bed. If he does not go back to bed, pick him up from behind so that he is facing away from you and cannot hug you. Immediately take him back to bed and say firmly, "Stay in your bedroom." You may need to do this over and over again before your child eventually stays in his room. Your child must realize that you are not going to give in and let him sleep in your room. If he calls out for you, follow the recommendations in the sidebar "Responding to Your Child's Frequent Calls for You."

The first night that you do this can be very tiring for you; therefore, make sure you do it on a night when you do not need to go to work the following day. Although the first several nights that you use this technique can be difficult, it can be effective. This technique works for a majority of parents within the first week and in many cases within the course of three to four nights. The first two nights are usually the worst.

Lying

It is very common for young children to lie. This is because young children have not yet learned that lying is wrong. Part of the reason that preschoolers lie is that they think of people as either good or bad. They also think that it is impossible for a good person to do something bad. Thus, to remain "good" in your eyes, your child may lie. For most young children, lying is not done mischievously but to protect them from punishment or disapproval. Therefore, use initial episodes of lying as an opportunity to teach rather than to punish.

Young children typically tell two types of lies. The first type is one that you would probably consider a "tall tale." In these cases, a child makes up a story that is not true, or he greatly exaggerates the truth. With younger children, these tall tales are often the product of their imagination and result from their inability to always know the difference between fantasy and reality. When your child is telling a tall tale, he is often expressing things that he wishes were true. When this occurs, it is usually best for you not to make a big deal about the tall tale but to matter-of-factly inject some reality into your child's story.

The second type of lie that young children often tell is one to obtain something they want or to avoid something. When this occurs, teach your child that lying is wrong and that it is important to tell the truth. Here are some ways of doing this:

- **Model truthfulness.** This is especially difficult when we frequently employ what we call "little white lies," which we think are OK. A parent might lie about her child's age at an amusement park or at a movie theater, or she might falsely tell someone that she has a prior commitment and cannot attend a function. When your child overhears you telling these lies, it is difficult for him to see them as different from lies that he tells. Therefore, try to be aware of and eliminate lying in front of your child.
- **Praise truthfulness.** Whenever your child is truthful about something he could have lied about, make sure that you praise him. Let him know you appreciate his truthfulness.
- **Explain to your child why telling the truth is important.** Start teaching your child the importance of telling the truth when he is very young. Also let him know that there are negative consequences for children who lie. In discussing lying, try to keep explanations as concrete as possible, and realize that children under the age of three or four are going to have difficulty comprehending the concept of lying. Give concrete examples of telling the truth and telling a lie.
- **Try to remain calm when your child is not telling the truth.** Don't yell or scream at your child when you recognize he is being untruthful. Losing your temper is not going to help the situation.

- **Do not let your child's lie work!** If your child lied in order to get something, make sure that he does not get it.
- **Try to be consistent in how you handle lying.** Have a consistent rule about lying and how to handle it. As your child grows older and knows that he is lying, there should be some consequence for lying (time-out or the removal of some privilege).
- **Avoid shaming your child for lying.** It is fine for you to let your child know you are disappointed with him when he lies. However, make sure that he realizes what you are disappointed about is that he lied and that you are not questioning his worth as an individual. Avoid labeling your child as a "liar."

Sibling Rivalry

Sibling rivalry occurs in all families with more than one child. It is normal, and, in fact, children learn valuable lessons about how to deal with and resolve conflict. When your children are pestering each other, try to realize that they are learning valuable lessons about social interactions. Your goal as a parent should not be to eliminate sibling rivalry but rather to minimize it. Sibling rivalry is usually strongest between same-sex siblings who are one to three years apart in age. We will examine two common times for sibling rivalry: following the birth of a new baby and as children grow older.

A New Baby

After the birth of a baby, many older siblings become jealous and may express some hostility toward their baby brother or sister. Other children may regress in their behavior. For example, if they have been toilet-trained, they start wetting or soiling themselves after the birth of a baby. Other children may react by withdrawing or by engaging in more attention-seeking behavior, such as becoming more fussy and demanding of their parents' time. This is difficult for parents as they are trying to meet the new demands of the baby. Fortunately, when you are expecting another child, you can take some steps to help your older child adapt to having a sibling and thus to minimize rivalry:

- **Prepare your child for what to expect.** Explain exactly what will happen when you are in the hospital and who will be taking care of him. Try to cover all of the details so he will not be worried. Also explain what a new baby will be like. Tell him that babies cry a lot and they also sleep a lot. Let him know that although you'll be spending a lot of time looking after the baby, you do not love him any less.
- **Let your child accompany you to prenatal visits and listen to the baby's heartbeat.** Involve your child in prenatal events that allow him to actively participate. Being able to listen to a heartbeat or see an ultrasound can help him realize a baby is really on the way.
- **If possible, make any significant changes in the home several months before the baby arrives.** If your child is using a crib that you plan to use for the baby, move the crib out of your child's room several months before the baby arrives. Make a big deal about your child getting a big kid's bed, rather than saying you are going to be using the crib for the baby. Also, if any room changes you plan to make will affect your child, make them well before your due date.
- **Avoid asking your child if he wants a baby brother or sister.** He has no choice in this matter! If he says "no," you are really going to be stuck.
- **It is usually best to wait to let your child know about your pregnancy until you are in the second trimester and the greatest risk of miscarriage has passed.** Miscarriages can be very difficult to explain to young children.
- **Try not to talk too much about the baby being a playmate for your older child.** It will be a long time before an infant is able to play with his older brother or sister. Your older child may become disappointed when the baby is born and cannot throw a ball or play other games right away.

- **Try not to undertake new developmental tasks with your child, such as toilet-training, around the time the baby is due.** If your child is not toilet trained, either start toilet training several months before your baby is due or wait until several months after the birth of the baby.

You can use the following recommendations after the new baby is born:

- **If possible, let your child see the baby in the hospital.** Check with the hospital to see if they have any specific visitation guidelines and/or programs for siblings.
- **Let your child help you with the baby.** Try to make it a pleasant experience for all of you by using frequent attends and praises with your older child when he is helping. If he does not want to help, do not force him.
- **Parents often make a big deal about taking baby photographs and having a baby book.** Bring out your older child's baby book to show him and to have on display after the baby is born. You also can make a family photograph album or scrapbook for your older child to let him know that he is just as special as the baby.
- **Make sure you spend time alone with your older child.** As you know, having a baby in the home is very demanding. Your older child can easily feel ignored. Find time to spend with your older child doing enjoyable activities that you have done with him in the past.
- **Do not ignore aggressive behavior.** If your child is aggressive toward the baby, you must deal with this behavior immediately by giving him time-outs. Of course, you also should praise your child for his positive behavior with the baby.

As Children Grow Older

As children grow older, sibling rivalry continues to be a very normal part of a sibling relationship. Often it occurs because the children are competing for their parents' attention, fighting over ownership of something, or trying to be seen as superior to each other in some way. The following recommendations can help you reduce sibling rivalry and minimize its negative effects:

- **It is impossible to treat your children totally equally.** However, you should try to communicate to them that you recognize their unique traits and acknowledge their individual accomplishments.
- **Try to spend time alone with each of your children regularly.** Try to have special yet different activities that you do with each child.
- **Acknowledge when your children do get along, especially in difficult situations where they could easily fight with each other.** Use your attending and praising skills.
- **Avoid comparing your children with one another.** Although each of your children has his strengths and weaknesses, it's very important that you do not compare children with each other in regard to these strengths and weaknesses.
- **Try to ignore minor conflict between your children.** Let them work it out on their own. Intervene only if the conflict becomes physical or excessive.
- **When your children are fighting, it is usually impossible to find out who started it.** Unless you saw exactly what happened and know that only one child was at fault, intervene with both children. In most cases both children contribute to a fight. Perhaps one hit first, but often the other child was teasing or provoking him. Do not try to talk about the fight when it is happening. First, put both children in time-out to give them a chance to calm down. The issue they were fighting about can be addressed later. Your immediate goal should be to separate the children and have them gain self-control. When you use time-out with two children at once, put them in separate time-out areas so they cannot continue fighting.
- **After time-out, use the conflict as a chance to teach the children more appropriate problem-solving skills.** Try to

have them identify the problem and ways that they can deal with the problem more effectively in the future. Younger children may need some suggestions. As children grow older, encourage them to generate suggestions on their own.

- **Try to ignore tattling.** A child often will come to his parents to tattle on his sibling when he feels that it may get the sibling in trouble. When tattling occurs, tell your child to go back to his sibling and try to work on the issue with him. You can acknowledge your child's feelings by saying something like, "I know that must make you very angry." You also can ask your child, "What do you think would be a good way for you to deal with . . . ?" Posing this type of problem-solving question will help your child think about how he can handle the issue.

Behavior Problems at Preschool/School

It should come as no surprise that the behavior of many strong-willed children is not only problematic at home but also at preschool/school. One of the keys to effectively addressing a child's behavior problem at school is for the parents to establish a strong relationship with their child's teacher. When a parent and teacher come together as a "team," they can be more successful. This success is often the result of frequent communication and shared behavior-management strategies between parents and teachers.

Here are some recommendations for parents regarding what they can do to help address behavior problems at school:

- **Schedule a meeting with your child's teacher at the beginning of the school year.** This meeting should be used to establish or strengthen your relationship with the teacher. Let the teacher know that you want to work together to help your child succeed in school.
- **Make sure you attend all regularly scheduled parent-teacher conferences.** Prepare for parent-teacher confer-

ences and other scheduled meetings with the teacher by making a list of questions you want to ask the teacher. Most questions should be focused on specific areas of concern such as:

"What do you see as my child's strengths and weaknesses?"

"What concerns do have about my child's behavior?"

"What ways have you found to be most effective in managing his behavior?"

"How is he doing in terms of learning skills (or class work)?"

"What can I do at home to help with his learning and behavior?"

- **Also prepare a list of things you want to tell the teacher about your child.** This list might include items such as:

Sharing what you have found most helpful in managing his behavior at home. You might want to share the strategies you learned from reading this book!

Sharing your thoughts about how you think your child learns best (e.g., auditory, visual).

Discuss any learning problems you suspect he might have.

- **Remember the communication skills we discussed in Chapter 13.** You can utilize these skills to facilitate the discussions you have with the teacher.

- **If your child is having significant problems at school, work with the teacher to develop an "action plan."** This plan should address the specific areas of concern and state exactly what both the teacher and parent are going to do to address the problems.

- **Have frequent "check-ins" with the teacher regarding your child's progress.** This might involve daily parent-teacher notes or regular e-mails or phone calls.

- **Reward your child for any reported improvements in school.** Follow the guidelines in Chapter 7 regarding the effective use of rewards.

Conclusion

We have provided some solutions to common problems experienced by parents of two- to six-year-old strong-willed children. Of course, a strong-willed child will display many other problems as well. But now you should be able to devise solutions to those problems by using the strategies discussed in this book.

Parenting, like any other activity, requires effort, planning, and problem solving. It is work, but it can be fun and rewarding.

Happy parenting!

Words to Remember

A hundred years from now it will not matter what sort of house I lived in, what my bank account was, or the kind of car I drove, but the world may be different because I was important in the life of a child.

—Author unknown

Appendix
Resources for Parents and Professionals

Resources provided in this section include a listing of recommended websites and books for parents as well as references/resources for professionals who would like additional information about our program.

Resources for Parents

Websites

Center for Effective Parenting
parenting-ed.org

This noncommercial website offers information on a variety of parenting topics. Go to the "Parent Handouts" section for practical suggestions on how to handle a variety of issues. There are also numerous handouts on issues related to children's learning and education.

Healthy Children
healthychildren.org

This website is sponsored by the American Academy of Pediatrics for parents. It provides information on topics including child development, health, safety, and family issues.

Parenting 24/7
parenting247.org

This University of Illinois website was developed to be a "one-stop" source of news, information, and advice on parenting. The website provides recent news articles related to parenting and children, feature articles written for parents on a wide variety of topics, as well as a large number of video clips of parents and professionals discussing parenting challenges and strategies.

CYFERnet
cyfernet.org

CYFERnet (Children, Youth and Families Education and Research Network) is offered through the national group of university-based Cooperative Extension System Programs. The purpose of this site is to provide professionals and parents with practical research-based information on a wide variety of topics related to children, youth, and families.

YourChild: Development and Behavior Resources
med.umich.edu/yourchild

This University of Michigan Health System website offers information on an extremely wide variety of topics related to child development, behavior, safety, and health issues.

Child and Family WebGuide
cfw.tufts.edu

This Tufts University website describes and evaluates other websites that contain research-based information on child development and parenting. Links to these sites are provided.

National Center for Fathering

fathers.com

This website offers a variety of information related to fathering. Topics include information specific to fathers as well as more general information on parenting.

Websites of Professional Organizations

The following national organization websites contain information that may be of interest to parents. Most of them have large sections of their websites devoted to child, parent, and family issues.

American Psychological Association

apa.org

American Academy of Pediatrics

aap.org

American Academy of Child and Adolescent Psychiatry

aacap.org

Association for Behavioral and Cognitive Therapies

abct.org

Books for Parents

The following books offer additional information for parents on selected topics we mention in *Parenting the Strong-Willed Child*.

Barkley, R. (2000). *Taking Charge of ADHD: The Complete, Authoritative Guide for Parents*. New York: Guilford Press.
Brooks, R., and S. Goldstein. (2002). *Raising Resilient Children: Fostering Strength, Hope, and Optimism in Your Child*. New York: McGraw-Hill.

Elkind, D. (2007). *The Power of Play: Learning What Comes Naturally.* Philadelphia: De Capo Press.

Ferber, R. (2006). *Solve Your Child's Sleep Problems: New, Revised, and Expanded Edition.* New York: Fireside.

Gottman, J., and N. Silver. (2000). *The Seven Principles for Making Marriage Work.* New York: Three Rivers Press.

Long, N., and R. Forehand. (2002). *Making Divorce Easier on Your Child: 50 Effective Ways to Help Children Adjust.* New York: McGraw-Hill.

References/Resources for Professionals

The following references may be of interest to professionals who would like additional information on our program. These references include information on the clinical intervention (Helping the Noncompliant Child) upon which the five-week parenting program is based as well as evaluation studies of our clinical program, our parenting class program, and the *Parenting the Strong-Willed Child* book itself.

Conners, N. A., M. C. Edwards, and A. S. Grant. (2007). "An Evaluation of a Parenting Class Curriculum for Parents of Young Children: *Parenting the Strong-Willed Child.*" *Journal of Child and Family Studies,* 16, 321–330.

Forehand, R. L., M. J. Merchant, N. Long, and E. Garai. (2010). "An Examination of *Parenting the Strong-Willed Child* as Bibliotherapy for Parents." *Behavior Modification,* 34, 57–76.

McMahon, R. J., and R. L. Forehand. (2003). *Helping the Noncompliant Child: Family-Based Treatment for Oppositional Behavior.* (2nd edition). New York: Guilford.

McMahon, R. J., N. Long, and R. Forehand (2010). "Parent Training for the Treatment of Oppositional Behavior in Young Children: Helping the Noncompliant Child." In R. Murrihy and T. Ollendick (eds.), *Handbook of Clinical Assessment and Treatment of Conduct Problems in Youth.* New York: Springer.

Parenting Class Curriculum Available

A Parenting Class Curriculum based on *Parenting the Strong-Willed Child* is available. The six two-hour-sessions class uses this book as a parent manual. Professionals who are interested in obtaining information about this resource should contact Dr. Nicholas Long at longnicholas@uams.edu.

Index

About the Authors

Rex Forehand, Ph.D., is University Distinguished Professor, Ansbacher Professor of Psychology, and director of clinical Training at the University of Vermont. Dr. Forehand, a child clinical psychologist, has devoted forty years to studying behavior problems of children and developing strategies for parents to use to change those problems. Furthermore, his research has addressed the role of the broader family environment (such as conflict between parents, divorce, parental depression, physical illness) and its influence on parenting and child behavior. His research and applied clinical programs have been published in more than 400 professional journal articles and book chapters. His book *Helping the Noncompliant Child* (written with Robert J. McMahon) has received national acclaim for its delineation of a proven clinical intervention program for therapists to use with parents of children with behavior problems. Dr. Forehand's book, *Making Divorce Easier on Your Child: 50 Effective Ways to Help Children Adjust* (McGraw-Hill) (written with Dr. Long), offers parents who are divorcing guidelines for enhancing their children's adjustment during this difficult time. Dr. Forehand's clinical and research efforts have resulted in his recognition as one of the most frequently cited authors in psychology, identification as one of the leading child mental health professionals in the United States, frequent citations in the public media, and appointment to many editorial boards of professional journals. He has received the following awards:

American Psychological Association's (APA) Distinguished Career Award for Clinical Child and Adolescent Psychology; APA's Distinguished Career Contributions to Education and Training Award; the Rivendell Foundation Award for Outstanding Contributions to Improving the Research and Delivery of Mental Health Services to Children and Adolescents; University of Vermont Scholar Award; and the William A. Owens Jr. Award for Creative Research in Social and Behavioral Sciences. Dr. Forehand is married, the father of two grown children, and a grandfather.

Nicholas Long, Ph.D., is a professor of pediatrics and the director of pediatric psychology at the University of Arkansas for Medical Sciences (UAMS) and Arkansas Children's Hospital. Dr. Long is also director of the Center for Effective Parenting, which provides services to thousands of parents each year. An extensively published scholar in the areas of parenting and family influences on child behavior, Long has published his research in leading professional journals and books. He also has been appointed to the editorial boards of many psychology professional journals in the fields of psychology and pediatrics. The primary focus of his work has been the development of strategies, materials, and programs in the area of parenting. His book, *Making Divorce Easier on Your Child: 50 Effective Ways to Help Children Adjust* (McGraw-Hill) (written with Dr. Forehand), draws on his expertise in the area of parental divorce and provides a practical guide for parents to use to promote the adjustment of children during and after divorce. He is coeditor (with Masud Hoghughi) of the *Handbook of Parenting: Theory and Research for Practice*, which is an international textbook for professionals. In addition to his clinical and research activities, Dr. Long plays an active role in training pediatricians and psychologists in the science and art of parenting. Dr. Long is an acclaimed public speaker whose parenting presentations are in great demand. He is a frequently requested keynote speaker on parenting topics at the regional, national, and international levels. Dr. Long is a recipient of the Rivendell Foundation Award for Outstanding Contributions to Improving the Research and Delivery of Mental Health Services to Children and Adolescents and the Arkansas Psychological Association's Distinguished Psychologist Award. He is also the recipient of numerous teaching awards including the UAMS College of Medicine's Educational Innovation Award and Educational Research Award, as well as the UAMS Chancellor's Faculty Teaching Award. He is married and the father of two sons.